AF792576

Divorce and Muslim Women

Divorce and Muslim Women

S.A.H. Moinuddin

Published under the auspices of
VIDYASAGAR UNIVERSITY, MIDNAPORE (W.B.)

Rawat Publications
Jaipur and New Delhi

ISBN 81-7033-557-6
© Author, 2000

No part of this book may be reproduced or transmitted in any form or by any means, electronic or mechanical including photocopying, recording or by any information storage and retrieval system without permission in writing from the publishers.

Published by
Prem Rawat for ***Rawat Publications***
3-Na-20, Jawahar Nagar, Jaipur 302 004 India
Phone: +91 141 651022 / 651438 Fax: +91 141 651748

Delhi Office
G-4, 4832/24, Ansari Road, Darya Ganj, New Delhi 110 002
Phone: 3263290

Typeset by Rawat Computers, Jaipur
Printed at Nice Printing Press, New Delhi

To my respected teachers

Professor SURAJIT CHANDRA SINHA
Former Vice Chancellor, Visva Bharati, Santiniketan,
Director, Anthropological Survey of India, and
Director, Centre for Studies in Social Sciences, Calcutta

and

Dr. SWAPAN KUMAR PRAMANICK
Professor of Sociology, University of Calcutta

my friends, philosophers and guides.

Contents

Foreword

There are two distinct perspectives that can be applied to the study of divorce in any society. One can focus on the corpus of legal rules defining the rights of the husband and wife in the event a divorce is contemplated, the rights the spouses enjoy with respect to children and property, and the procedure laid down for giving the seal of final authority to a divorce. Or, one can focus on divorce as a sociological phenomenon and explore the processes that are set in motion once the stability of marriage is threatened and divorce takes place. In the latter case, the emphasis is on the factors that contribute to breakdown of marriages, the role that kinsmen and social relations play in trying to work towards a possible reconciliation between the estranged spouses, the procedure that is followed for giving effect to a divorce and the consequences that follow for the spouses, and particularly women, as a result of the divorce. This perspective does not treat divorce in isolation, but tries to look at it in the wider context of social structure.

Dr. Syed Abdul Hafiz Moinuddin's monograph is a study

of divorce among Muslims of West Bengal in terms of the second perspective. He examines in the light of painstakingly collected empirical evidence from two *gram panchayats*, in the Barddhaman and Murshidabad districts, the incidence of divorce and separation, the manner in which divorce takes place, the social and other causes due to which the practice of divorce and separation persists, and the position of divorced and separated women in society. As Muslims claim to follow the *Quran* and are bound by the Muslim Personal Law, Dr. Moinuddin is led to deal with the *Quranic* and legal injunctions relating to divorce and the extent to which they are actually adhered to in practice. Quite often, the adherence of Muslims to the religious prescriptions and formal legal codes is taken for granted. It is assumed that their practices are shaped by what religion and law formally lay down. It is hardly ever contemplated that their social practices may be a reflection of more immediate existential pressures and conditions rather than of the formal codes laid down by the *Quranic* or Muslim Personal Law. Dr. Moinuddin's effort to examine the degree of congruity between the *Quranic* injunctions and legal codes is to be commended as it has the potential to show how there is often a wide gap between religious theory and social practice.

Dr. Moinuddin's monograph has an immediate practical relevance as well. For some years, the Muslim law of divorce, particularly the provision of triple divorce which vests a unilateral right upon the husband to pronounce a summary divorce upon his wife by simply stating three times at one sitting that he is divorcing her, has been a subject of considerable controversy. On one side, those opposed to the practice of triple divorce---and this includes chauvinist and liberal Hindus as well as liberal Muslims—argue that the legal provision allowing a Muslim husband to pronounce divorce upon his wife at one go renders the position of a Muslim woman extremely weak and vulnerable. On the other side, those opposed to any change in Muslim Personal Law reason that divorce rates are extremely low among Muslims in India and the assertion that Muslim divorce practices render the position of Muslim women particularly weak is without substance. Both positions have been pressed into the controversy without any effort to ascertain the empirical situation. Dr. Moinuddin's monograph represents the first serious attempt to ascertain and present the facts as they obtain on the ground and to empirically evaluate the position of divorced and separated Muslim women.

Certain complexities are involved in dealing with divorce in Muslim communities. The first of these relates to the divergence that crystallised historically and currently prevails between what may be described as the revealed injunctions in the *Quran* and those injunctions that came to be subsequently articulated in varied ways in the jurisprudences enunciated by the different schools of Muslim law. If the revealed text was quite as explicit as average Muslims commonly believe is truly the case, there would indeed have been no basis for this kind of variation to prevail. Yet, the fact of the situation is that such variation currently exists, leading to a curious situation that one can talk in the same breath, as it were, of a *Quranic* law and Muslim Personal Law. The two are not necessarily consonant, not at least on many points in respect of divorce practices. Formal Muslim scholarship has not been successful in dealing and coming to terms with this dichotomy, which continues to prevail even today, and is, to a considerable extent, unresolvable because the revealed injunctions are either self-contradictory (one revealed injunction cancels out another) or are not sufficiently precise so as to rule out conflicting interpretation. This has resulted in an unhappy and uncomfortable situation where despite each school of Islamic law claiming to derive its authority from the *Quran* interprets it differently in a way that a diversity of forms and formal procedures is allowed to prevail in respect of divorce practices among different Muslim communities.

Popular Muslim belief is likely to view such an assertion as blasphemous, or at least as a gross misrepresentation of the true Islamic spirit. But that is not so because the dichotomy is not real and does not exist in reality. It is so because average Muslims do not have a sufficiently deep understanding of the *Quran* and have generally constituted their beliefs about what the Quran prescribes on the basis of what they have been told by those who claim to have a degree of knowledge of the *Quran*. No useful purpose will be served by going into the question as to how informed or reliable their own understanding is. What needs to be noted is that those claiming access to and command over the revealed injunctions choose to press and pass on what according to their belief and interpretation is the message and prescription of the *Quran*. As a consequence, an average Muslim grows up believing that what his preacher (*maulvi, pesh imam, or alim*) has taught him is the true message of Islam. He, at no point, seeks to match what his preacher has taught him with what the *Quranic* text itself enunciates in reality either because he has no access to the latter or lacks the authority to challenge institutionalised scholastic opinion which is supposed to be the virtual monopoly of the trained clerics (*alims* in the first instance and by extension *maulvis and pesh imams* who constitute the agencies directly responsible for dissemination of Islamic beliefs and values to the common mass of Muslims). For this obvious reason, which links up with the larger and deeper question of how an average Muslim is socialised into Islamic beliefs and values in the first place, the variation between what we described as *Quranic* law and Muslim Personal Law is able to prevail widely in Muslim communities.

Of course, this situation is not without its positive dimensions. One positive consequence flowing out of it is that a basis is created for dialogue and debate and for public opinion to be mobilised in favour of reform of social practices that are considered to be either oppressive or unfair towards those adversely affected by an aspect of the legal code as it is sought to be imposed by those claiming institutionalised standing to be the sole arbiters of either *Quranic* injunctions or Muslim Personal Law. For over a century, there has been repeated public pressure for changes in divorce practices and issues arising out of them. The first time such public pressure resulted in modification of the law relating to divorce was with respect to the period for which a woman, whose husband had disappeared and whose whereabouts were not known, had to wait before she could contract another marriage. Under *Hanafi* law which governs the large majority of Muslim in the Indian subcontinent, she was required to wait for a period of 99 years before she could contemplate contracting a second marriage. Obviously, the practice was severely oppressive and public pressure was mobilised to change the legal position in accordance with the considerably liberal *Quranic* position adopted by other schools of Muslim Personal Law. Again, over the past several decades public pressure has been building up in favour of a modification of the Muslim practice of triple divorce (unilateral repudiation of marriage at one siting by the husband without any formal social intervention) which *Hanafi* law allows as legally tenable and binding on the wife and her kinsmen. The proponents of change rely upon the *Quranic* injunctions as against the *Hanafi* law to buttress their claim for a change in this procedure for divorce. Evidence brought together by Dr. Moinuddin on the situation and plight of divorced and separated women should serve to demonstrate the imperative for such change.

The second complexity relates to the problem involved in the operation of *khula* divorce where the wife is allowed to ask for the dissolution of marriage. Traditionalist Muslim opinion tries to make a great deal of this legal provision, claiming that Muslim Personal Law is so equitous that it even allows woman the right to divorce her husband. Even though the right is technically guaranteed to a Muslim woman, its exercise is in reality hemmed in by enormous difficulties. A Muslim husband retains the power to veto her demand. Women can give effect to this right only by appealing to the good sense of the husband or by bringing pressure on the husband to consent to a divorce. If he is vindictive and adamant, which is quite frequently the case in reality, she has no means of freeing herself from the marital bond. Dr. Moinuddin's data show that there are many cases of *khula* divorce among the women he interviewed, but he does not provide any evidence to indicate how easy or complicated it was for them to secure divorce and what strategies they had to employ to secure *khula* divorce. One wishes Dr. Moinuddin had discussed a few cases of women who have obtained *khula* divorce so that this point could be clarified.

The third complexity relates to the contradiction arising out of the imperative to adhere to the *Quranic* principles and the continuing influence of Indian cultural ethos in the life of Indian Muslims. Even though every Muslim in India (and this holds for Muslims everywhere) claims adherence to the *Quran* (and therefore to the Islamic *sharia'*), the truth is that on many aspects his attitudes and behaviour deviate from the *Quranic* norms because of the continuing hold of cultural orientations and practices that enjoy legitimacy in the Indian environment. For example, the *Quranic* position in respect of divorce is relatively accommodating. Even though exhorting continuity of a marital union as desirable, the *Quran* does provide for divorce in accordance with the principles of fairplay and gender justice. There is no social stigma against divorce and a divorced women is not subjected to any kind of stigma for having either asked for divorce or for having been divorced by her husband. Even so, because of the continuing hold of indigenous values divorce is looked down upon in Muslim communities in India and the divorced woman is also subjected to some kind of social stigma on that count. Of course, one is not arguing that the negative attitudes towards divorce and divorced women are uniform throughout Indian society and among all social communities and classes. There is undoubtedly a great deal of variation across social communities and classes. Negative attitudes towards divorced and divorced women are probably the strongest among higher and intermediate castes and social classes and tend to be greatly attenuated as one moves down the social hierarchy. The point one is making is that Muslim attitudes towards divorce and separation reflect to some degree the influence of dominant indigenous values, and their attenuation down the hierarchy of Muslim social groups closely follows the pattern among other social communities and groups. This is clearly indicated by Dr. Moinuddin's finding that the incidence of divorce and separation is higher among Muslims of lower social strata.

There is a widespread belief which has been reinforced by the current controversy over the practice of triple divorce that the incidence of divorce tends to be high among Muslims because the Muslim Personal Law is gender unjust on the subject and allows the man the freedom to exercise his right of divorce without having to account for his action. While it is true that there is an obvious gender discrimination in Muslim Personal Law which has the potential to favour men, the evidence brought forth by Dr. Moinuddin shows that divorce has to be seen within a larger social framework which takes account of the social structure, economic conditions and cultural values of the families. His own data suggests that divorce is more prevalent among low status and income strata. Even though he does not analyse the deeper dynamics of what it is about low status and income that contributes to a higher incidence of divorce, he may not be far wrong in arguing that "the position of the divorced and separated Muslim women in West Bengal is low. In general, they come from low income families, with their guardians and husbands struggling for a hand-to-mouth existence. Not only are the income levels low, but also their families are more often than not, engaged in the so-called low status occupations". He concludes, therefore, that any improvement of the status of divorced and separated women "demands positive attacks on poverty, literacy and social restrictions which presuppose male superiority and dominance".

Muslim Personal Law obliges a Muslim woman to observe the statutory period of seclusion (considered necessary to establish the paternity of a child she might be carrying) and gives her the right to dower (*mahr*) in the event of divorce. Dr. Moinuddin's data suggests that these obligations are observed more in their violation. If this finding is correct, and I find no reason to doubt its validity in the light of my own and others researches among Muslims in other parts of India, an obvious conclusion would seem to be that the powerful patriarchal orientations prevalent in society are a more critical determinant of the disadvantaged situation of divorced and separated Muslim women than the ideals enjoined upon Muslims by their faith. Where the law is gender unjust, as indeed it is in respect of allowing men the unilateral right to pronounce divorce upon his wife without assigning any reason, it is used to their advantage and convenience and their action is rationalised on the ground that it is sanctioned by their religion and legal codes. Where the law is strict, as indeed it is in respect of guaranteeing divorced women the right to dower (*mahr*) and dowry (*jahez*) as well as property, it is violated with impunity to put the women to a disadvantage and to suit male interests. Clearly, any campaign for an improvement in the status of Muslim women should not address itself only to removing those lacunae in laws which capricious men can use to justify their action. It would simultaneously have to address itself to ensuring that adherence to rules that protect the rights of women is made mandatory for men by the very act of divorce pronounced by them. The divorce pronounced unilaterally by a man should become final after the man has discharged his legal responsibilities of paying the dower or returning the dowry to his wife. Only when this is made obligatory that the evil of triple divorce can be adequately addressed.

Dr. Moinuddin deserves appreciation for producing a research monograph on a subject about which we have so far had no empirical knowledge. One hopes that his book will stimulate similar research among Muslim communities in other parts of the country so that a fairly representative picture of the institution of divorce among Muslims is able to emerge.

Imtiaz Ahmad

Acknowledgements

The present work has been sponsored by the Indian Council of Social Science Research (ICSSR), New Delhi. Professor Surajit Chandra Sinha, former Vice Chancellor of Visva Bharati University, Director of the Anthropological Survey of India and the Centre for Studies in Social Sciences, Calcutta, was kind enough to supervise my fieldwork and various phases of preparating present work. I express my deepest and sincere gratitude to him as my supervisor.

I am greatly indebted to the authority of Vidyasagar University for subsidising the publication of my Ph.D. thesis out of the UGC unassigned grant allotted in favour of the university.

My sincere thanks are due to Professor Imtiaz Ahmad of Jawaharlal Nehru University, New Delhi who has taken pains to write a foreword to the present publication.

Shri Anjan Ghosh, Fellow of the Centre for Studies in Social sciences, Calcutta, helped me a lot in probing deeply into the problem. I must remember him with gratitude. My thanks are also due to Shri Siddhartha Mazumdar, Lecturer, City College, Amherst Street, Calcutta and Dr. Prabir Kumar Kundu, Department of Applied Mathematics with Oceanology and Computer Programming, Vidyasagar University, who helped me a lot in organising the data.

I owe much to the renowned *Kisan* leaders, late Abdullah Rasul and late Abdul Mansur Habibullah, Shri Sukanti Dutta, Lecturer, City College, Surya Sen Street, Calcutta, with whom I had very frank discussions about my field data and received excellent responses. I am grateful to Shri Satya Gopal Sinha, Headmaster, Billagram High School of Barddhaman district and Dr. Sankar Prasad Sinha, Reader, Department of English, Vidyasagar University, who went through the manuscripts and gave important suggestions.

I pay my deep regards to my teacher, Professor Swapan Kumar Pramanick of the Department of Sociology, University of Calcutta and my respected colleague, Professor Tarun Kumar Banerjee of the Department of Political Science with Rural Administration, Vidyasagar University for their valuable suggestions, sympathy, encouragement and guidance in my present endeavour.

I am greatly indebted to Professor Bela Dutta Gupta (Retd.), Professor Swapan Kumar Bhattacharya, Dr. Krishna Chakraborty and Dr. Bholanath Banerjee of the Department of Sociology, University of Calcutta for their valuable suggestions and comments on my research study which have undoubtedly enriched the horizon of my knowledge in this regard.

I record my deep gratitude to the two brothers, Qazi Mahiuddin Haque and Qazi Anwarul Haque of Mongolkote, Barddhaman district and the two brothers Kamaluddin Hyder and Sahabuddin Hyder of Panchthupi, Murshidabad district for providing me with accommodation and all kinds of help at the time of my fieldwork. I also take the opportunity to acknowledge the assistance received from all the respondents of both the Mongolkote Gram Panchayat of Barddhaman district and the Panchthupi Gram Panchayat of Murshidabad district. They provided me with relevant information and tendered their sincere cooperation.

I am indebted to my wife Bilkis Anowar and my sons Master Syed Wasif alias Rohon, Syed Tausif alias Rayan and my niece Ulfat Ara alias Ripa for their unfailing support and adding cheer to my endeavour.

Then my thanks are also due to Biswajit Sarkar, Electro Type, Burdge Town, Midnapore for typing the manuscripts.

In a nutshell, I offer my respectful complements to all concerned who offered a helping hand in collecting data and preparing this work.

Syed Abdul Hafiz Moinuddin

1

Introduction

The year 1975 was declared as the "International Year for Women" by the United Nations to highlight the problems faced by half of the humanity throughout the globe. Subsequently, the period 1975-85 was designated as the "U.N. World Decade for Women: Equality, Development and Peace". It was in this decade that most governments accepted the integration of women in the society in general as an objective, and a number of countries introduced some new constitutional and legislative provisions to guarantee equal rights to them. In this decade, the women's question acquired a new dimension and momentum.

The appointment of the National Committee on the Status of Women in India[1] in 1972 and the publication of its report in 1975 marked the first official attempt to study the status of Indian women and recommend some steps or measures to improve their position. It has been pointed out that despite constitutional guarantees the roles, rights and participation of women in economic, social and political life are limited.

Thereafter, no national level committee has been appointed to reassess the achievement of the Women's Decade. Nonetheless, several reports have been formulated and none has given any encouraging picture.

There are several ways one can look at the status of women in any society. During the last decade, if we take note of the studies done on Indian Muslim women, we find that they relied more on prescriptive norms than on empirical facts and so generalisations have remained factually inadequate. The idea commonly held is that women, especially women in Muslim society, are a most neglected lot---having a miserable social status and hardly any opportunities to develop their personality. But this condition of women is not peculiar to any particular religion. Throughout the world, women, irrespective of their religions, are denied equal rights and opportunities in education, employment and participation in economic, political and social activities as compared to men. Very naturally, this situation generates and perpetuates a marked gender-biased social discrimination against women, in general, and Muslim women, in particular. This leads to a couple of assumptions first, women suffer irrespective of their ancestral tradition and background; and secondly, there is a scope for ameliorating their lot by effective legislative, educational, economic and social reforms. Only then can deteriorating conditions of Indian women be changed. And to do that, we have to remove the general, though unfortunate, impression that women, especially Muslim women, are an expendable asset, a commodity.

A number of scholars have argued that the main reason behind such impression of Indian Muslim women is that while a considerable body of empirical research has been done on social institutions in India during the last two decades, both the quantum and range of sociological information on Muslims in India continue to remain scanty. It is, indeed, so scanty that writers of entirely opposed persuasions have found it possible to argue their conflicting positions without much difficulty. Furthermore, the relative paucity of dependable sociological data about the social institutions, religious beliefs and attitudes and values of the Muslims has allowed a wide variety of popular stereotypes about them to persist, and to be argued out.[2]

So, for having a correct picture of the social scenario, we need to analyse the existing literature dealing with Muslim women and the question of their status. The proliferation of women's studies over the last decades in India was largely concerned with the question of reforms and occupations. And these reforms neither aimed at improving the status of women in the family, nor in the society as a whole. But in the absence of any palpable structural changes, reforms and establishment of girls' schools could benefit only a small section of middle class Muslim women having the resources to take advantage of the legal reforms and educational facilities.[3]

Sociologists and social anthropologists have paid comparatively little attention to the study of women's position in Muslim society in our country. Imtiaz Ahmad[4] has rightly opined that while we know something about the structural and organizational characteristics of specific Muslim groups, there is little sociological information on the social framework within which Muslim groups operate. S.M. Raza[5] has also mentioned about the scarcity of sociological literature on Indian Muslims. He argues that the studies conducted so far on Indian Muslims by different scholars of other branches of knowledge have either been partial or one sided in scope or historical and non-sociological in approach. Similarly, M. Indu Menon[6] observes that no systematic effort has been made so far to find out the factors behind the low status of Muslim women. She further argues that the theme of social status of Muslim women has comparatively been a neglected field of study in Indian sociology. Imtiaz Ahmad, along with some other scholars, has edited a series of books on social stratification, religion, rituals, kinship, marriage and trends of modernization among the Muslims in India. But even in these volumes, the social problems of Muslim women like divorce, separation, etc., are ignored. Siddiqui[7] aptly holds the following view:

> The whole body politic which projects and sustains a certain framework of value in a society, that attempts to explain various social issues including the status of women and the underlying ideological theoretical assumptions, has never been seriously questioned in India by any critical studies on women.

Regarding the general sociological studies of Indian women, Beteille[8] observed:

> There is no dearth of discussion on what may be called the women's question in India. But, in absence of systematic studies, this discussion often leads to opposite conclusions, and indeed, it often starts from opposite assumptions about the position of women in Indian society.

He further argues:

> There are equally sharp differences of opinion about the changes taking place in the position of women in India. Some regard these changes as profound and pervasive... others maintain that the position of women has changed very little and that Indian society continues by and large to be a male-dominated society.

So we may say that sociological researches on women had previously focused almost exclusively on conflicts among the middle class working women. After 1975, there was a push to broaden the base of knowledge of low income rural and urban women. Economists, historians, demographers, lawyers and political scientists joined the sociologists to constitute a broad base of expertise and knowledge about the status and need of women. Similarly, researches on women are no longer seen as simply theoretical in nature, but are becoming increasingly policy-oriented as the need for public action is getting recognized.

It is worthwhile to mention in this regard that with the

gradual upswing of sociological interest in Muslim women some well-known sociologists have conducted a few studies on Indian Muslims from a sociological point of view. Some of them have dealt with the conditions, roles and status of Indian Muslim women and the changes taking place therein. Some of them have tried to examine their theoretical position vis-à-vis reality. A synoptic view of analyses made by some of these studies would throw some light on Indian Muslim women.

The Status of Muslim Women in North India by Shibani Roy[9] is based on the data collected during the years 1970-72 from the two cities of Delhi and Lucknow, which are understood to have the Muslim way of life typical of North India. The main reasons behind the selection of these two cities are cited as follows:

> The two cities are the two large metropolitan centres of the northern region of India, and reveal fairly sharply the changes occurring in the urban living pattern. The two cities, due to their geographical nearness, show marked similarities, more or less representing the Muslim way of life of the northern region of India. Besides, they have a long and established Islamic heritage. Lucknow was the capital of Avadh and had a Muslim ruler, *Shia* by faith. Delhi formed the capital of the Moghul sultanate and was ruled by the Moghuls who were *Sunni* by faith. *Shias* and *Sunnis* form the two most dominant religious sects in India. Investigating the *Shias* of Lucknow and *Sunnis* of Delhi provides a fair representation of these two major sections of Muslims.[10]

In both cities, the most densely populated Muslim areas were selected for the study—the area around Jama Masjid in Delhi and the entire Chowk area in Lucknow. The sample survey consisted of 300 families, 150 from Delhi and Lucknow each, which were selected at random with none of the families being related to each other. Roy collected her data from *Sayyad, Shaikh, Mughal and Pathan* families, belonging to the income group of Rs. 400-Rs. 1,000 per month. According to the author, these named categories have not been seen as hierarchical or as lineage or as social groups, but merely as named categories. Employing both interview schedules and observation techniques, Roy has assessed the position of women from the perspectives of *purdah* (veil; seclusion), education, marriage which are common to all the named categories. She has considered the quality of changes that have occurred in the Muslim families within three generations and their effects on the status of Muslim women. Her main intention has been to trace out the factors which have penetrated into and affected the family life and role patterns of the Muslim women. She has also considered the status of Muslim women in the context of their role as mothers and grandmothers.

After conducting her field survey, Shibani Roy concludes that with changes in the social milieu the attitude of Muslim men has gradually changed and now they want women to participate in more areas of social life, which were closed to them earlier. Regarding *purdah*, she has opined that *purdah* has become an indispensable part of the Muslim social structure because high status has long been accorded to families which observe it. The Prophet ordered the women of his family and tribe (*Quraish*) to use the *chadar* in public in order to distinguish them from those of other families. She then argues that in time this trait of the *Sayyad* women was taken up by other families. On the other hand, the use of *chadar* not only meant segregating the females from males but implied high breeding and high family status. Over the years *purdah* has become a status symbol and throughout history we get instances showing the various measures taken by the Muslim elite to protect and shield their women from being seen by the general public. In India, these features were adopted by the general Muslim mass consisting of local converts aspiring for a higher social status.

Roy has tried to identify the main reasons behind the observance of *purdah*. She argues:

> In the home environ, it appears that the important factor contributory to the conforming behaviour of the women is the role of the Muslim men in the capacity of girl's father, brother or pro-

> spective husband. It is their intervention and insistence that keeps the Muslim women bound to traditional behaviour. In this respect even the liberating influence of education has been severely handicapped. The Muslim father, on the one hand, is desirous of educating his daughter and, on the other, afraid that his educated daughter might flout tradition which would make it difficult for him to arrange her marriage. A further complication is that the future son-in-law might be traditional and might object to the liberty given to the girl in regard to *purdah*.[11]

She further asserts:

> There appears to be a tendency amongst Muslims to associate women with the basic instincts of men and hence so much care at secluding them. Besides, the men insist on the fidelity of the women, and *purdah* is the outcome of the masculine effort at laying low the female spirit of independence.[12]

The presence and prevalence of *purdah* in the Muslim social structure is there because Muslim women have been assigned a subordinate role by men and their adherence to the norms of *purdah* restricts and limits their roles, and thus brings down their social status. She concludes that often education works to produce a more rigid orthodoxy in the attitude of some women towards *purdah*, who then quote from the scriptures in defence of their stand on the *purdah* system. This custom has a tremendous influence on a Muslim woman's life. It has not only secluded her physically, but also mentally from the rest of the world, reducing her entire world to the *aangan* (courtyard) and *dalan* of the *jenana khana* (female quarters).

While considering women's place in family economy, the author argues that the choice of careers for Muslim women becomes very limited, and they are rarely given the liberty to select a job of their own choice. Teaching in a women institution is considered to be the most honourable occupation for women. The persistence of traditional norms like segregation of men and women reflects the unchanged character of this community and the reason for its slow progress. But, peculiarly enough, the Muslim women retain their authority within the domestic sphere by taking up more responsible roles. The reason for this, she says, is that the men try to compensate for the lack of opportunity given to the women outside their home by allotting them more responsible roles within the family. The author further argues that the basic level of women's participation in family financial decisions is comparatively higher than that of the male due to some traditional reasons. This high status of women with respect to the family finances is further elevated with the increase in their education and employment.

Regarding religion, the author states that Muslim women are more religiously inclined than men. But there is a difference between the present generation and the older one. Women, due to their better educational attainment, do not necessarily follow the rituals blindly now, but try to understand the holy book—the *Quran* with the result that they are more knowledgeable about Islam than older generations. The author also mentions that the Prophet did bring positive changes in the status of women in Arabia. But in India, repeated interpolations and misinterpretations by the *maulanas* (clergy) have changed the ideology of Islam, thus jeopardising the existing climate of change, as opposed to that of its Arabian counterpart. The picture of the existing conditions of the Muslim women in India partly substantiates this view.

In 1974, M. Indu Menon[13] conducted a study of the Muslims in four districts of Kerala—Malapuram, Calicut, Palghat and Cannore to ascertain the status of Muslim women in all these districts. On the basis of a simple random sample method, 450 women and 150 men, representing both rural and urban settings of the four districts with a comparatively high educational background were interviewed.

The main objective of Menon's study was to see whether education played a significant role in raising the social status of Muslim women. Given this perspective, she has sought to identify the factors and forces responsible for inhibiting status enhancement of the women in spite of education.

The author has divided her book, *Status of Muslim Women*, into nine chapters dealing with the theoretical framework, methodology and research settings; educational background of the respondents; marriage and family; economic and educational background, political and social background, attitude and behaviour of male respondents and conclusions with the summary of her findings.

In her book, the author has tried to find out the role of education in raising the status of Muslim women. In case it has contributed in their status, she has tried to probe the specific areas in which the improvement is discernible and apparent. If, on the other hand, education has not played any role in improving the status of these women, she has tried to identify the factors and forces responsible for inhibiting their status improvement in spite of education.

The author has presented data to show that in every major institutional sphere education has played a major role in raising the status of Muslim women. She finds that factors responsible for hindering educational attainment remain active and forcibly continue to keep the position of women low in society. She has cited two reasons for the low education levels among Muslim women, i.e., the lack of meaningful roles for educated women in the community and the practice of seclusion (*pardah*). Then, according to her, the institution of marriage and family are also obstacles in the improvement of the position of Muslim women. The traditional role of the wife and mother in a Muslim family and the very practices revolving around marriage compel the Muslim women to be entirely dependent upon men as well as hinder their educational achievement.

In the economic and occupational field, the position of Muslim women continues to be subordinate to men. Then also, seclusion in the house leaves them utterly dependent on the husbands in the matter of use and disposal of their property. As they are not expected to perform any occupation outside the home, Muslim society in general underestimates women's education. However, Menon finds that in spite of the traditionally ascribed subordinate position of Muslim women education has been able to contribute significantly to raising their social status. The higher the education of the respondents, the more modern is their attitude and behaviour and the higher their status in the society.

The author has tried to understand the status of Muslim women from a single variable point, but she fails to fully depict an in-depth and detailed picture of women's life in Muslim society.

Talat Ara Ashrafi[14] has studied the Muslim women of urban areas. She has tried to find out how far the attitudes and outlook of Muslim families are faith or tradition-oriented and how far reason-oriented. The author has also tried to find out the actual behaviour and practice of socio-cultural life among the Muslims in urban areas and the impact of education on Muslim women. According to her, Indian society is undergoing transformation because of various forces and factors like modern secular education, social legislation, etc. This process of social transformation is all-embracing and covers our total life. One significant impact of this process of transformation are the changes taking place in the status, role and behaviour pattern of Muslim women. To explore the actual behaviour, manners and mode of life of the urbanised Muslims in the existing socio-cultural milieu, and finally the impact of education on Muslim women, the author has selected the city of Patna in Bihar for collecting data as Patna is believed to be inhabited by people of different origins having different socio-cultural backgrounds.

She has selected family as unit of analysis interviewing 300 families. From each family one married woman has been selected for collecting relevant information. The author has used 'convenient sampling' as a technique of data collection because the selection of families and then of the respondents as the units of the sample was done on the basis of purpose and convenience of the investigator. For this purpose, the author has divided the city of Patna into three broad areas for her investigation—i.e., Patna city (the eastern part of the city settled during the ancient and medieval period and still the seat of Hindu-Muslim unity), Bankipore (the town settled during British regime and located in the middle region) and New Patna (the southern and western parts of the city settled mainly after independence). These three parts of the city of Patna reflect three different socio-cultural backgrounds of the inhabitants. It is in this backdrop, the author has selected 100 respondents from each of the three parts. So, the families and, hence, the respondents belonging to different *mohallas*, caste, income groups, educational levels and occupational backgrounds were selected after great objective considerations and research conveniences.

The whole study is divided into eight chapters dealing with theoretical framework, social settings, patterns of studies, marriage and family, education, *purdah*, family planning and future prospects as enumerated beforehand.

In her study, the author argues that in every major institutional sphere, there have been changes from traditionalism to modernity or from conservatism to rationality. She opines that the Muslim society is passing through a transitional phase of tradition-modernity interaction with a view to maintaining the real Islamic tilt. According to her, the Indian Muslim women are guided by religious sanctions and religious orientation to a considerable degree. The degree of social liberty and freedom enjoyed by the women of other religious communities are absent in case of Muslim women. Deviations from Islamic *Sharia* are found, but this cannot be branded as non-Islamic or anti-Islamic on the part of Muslim women. It is due to the ignorance of religious doctrines, certain constraints and external pressures that deviations have occurred. It is the lack of proper education and paucity of proper sources of information that have been greatly instrumental in their adherence to conservative norms and values, attitudes and opinions and shirking of participation in the life outside the home. Regarding family planning, the author finds Muslim women are no less conscious of the necessity of family planning and planned parenthood than their Hindu counterparts. They are well aware of the dangers of unplanned parenthood to the family as well as to the nation.

So we may argue that in the all-India context these studies are very scarce in numbers. Though, in recent times, many books and articles have come into existence, dealing with Muslims in general and Muslim women in particular in India, these can hardly be called to be a representative study of the Indian Muslim women in the contemporary context because all these studies are rather descriptive in nature, and as such are merely historical account. On the other hand, most of them are microsociological studies limited in scope with time and space. There is a dearth of a comprehensive sociological study based on field data and covering the various aspects of the problem, i.e., divorce and separation of Muslim women in general. Most of the authors have chosen one or the other aspects according to their own choice and convenience. Some important social problems of Indian Muslim women have thus been ignored by sociologists and social anthropologists.

In West Bengal, too, there is marked scarcity of sociological inquiry on the Muslim community or on its womenfolk. Rafiuddin Ahmad,[15] in his book, has depicted the complexities of the social structure of the community. Ranjit Kumar Bhattacharya[16] has worked on the changing social structure and cultural pattern of the Muslim of rural Bengal. The author has collected his data from villages in Birbhum district in West Bengal. But he too has engaged himself with the question of castes and similar divisions among the Muslims. M.K.A. Siddiqui[17] has studied the caste-like divisions among the Muslims in Calcutta. But no sociological inquiry has been made on Muslims as a whole, and particularly on the divorced and separated Muslim women in West Bengal.

It is to be noted here that Muslim women, in general, and divorced and separated Muslim women of West Bengal, in particular, are part of the wider socio-cultural complex which makes their position and condition somewhat inequitable. But in spite of the religious binding of Muslim women, changes have been occurring among them. Criticising the Muslim society for its static nature. Zarina Bhatty[18] acknowledges:

> The broad crust of static attitudes dominating the Muslim society has cracked ... and stirrings of progress are closely visible.

These changes and the reasons behind these changes should be noticed to get a clear picture of the basic reality. For we all know that there is a wide divergence between religious scriptures and their practice. "What is beyond doubt", Bhatty concludes, "is that once exposed to modern education, Muslim women not only change themselves, but become ardent advocates of change."

If it is so, then it is wrong to presume that *Sharia* has shaped totally the social life of Muslims in India as well as West Bengal. In this regard Imtiaz Ahmad[19] rightly observes:

> Muslims in India display an enormous variety in their social organization, religious beliefs and attitudes and values, and that sociological enquiries should be directed towards exploring this bewildering variety as well as to assessing the relative influence of the religious code and the wider socio-cultural complexes upon their social institutions and behaviour.

It means any attempt to study the divorced and separated Muslim women in West Bengal must start from the social framework in which they live. Their cultural milieu, socio-economic conditions, relationship with wider society, etc. are not only important for their improved position and betterment, but also for the progress of the community as a whole. Its social structure, cultural norms and value judgements are important determinants of the situation of Muslim women. Social traditions, practices as well as values exert major influences in shaping the attitudes as well as behavioural patterns of human beings at large. Emerging trends of any society cannot be viewed in isolation from them.

For this, any critical assessment and analysis of divorced and separated Muslim women in West Bengal must depend on the social framework. Social structure, cultural norms and value judgements influence social expectations regarding the behaviour of both men and women and determine their position in society. It is also to be noted that normative standards do not change at the same pace as changes in other forms of social organisation.

Education is the pre-condition and first step towards women's progress and any kind of development. It is, of course, a very sure way of inculcating independence, self-reliance and dignity in women. Awareness of the importance of good education for girls in itself is a sign of positive social change. Education does not mean being able to read and write or obtain degrees or diplomas. It exposes a person to the external world, enriches and refines his sensibility to external forces. The Indian situation was such towards the end of the last century that it was not easy to find out more than one educated woman in Presidency towns of Bombay, Calcutta and Madras. If we take note of 1901 census, we find that the rate of female literacy was 0.69 per cent. At the beginning of this century, only women of the upper strata were allowed to receive formal education. That was culturally and religiously desirable and was obtained under private instruction. Initially, there were no special institutional provisions of education for women.

Since independence, however, the percentage of female literacy has been increasing steadily. It increased from 7.93 per cent in 1951 to 24.88 per cent in 1981. As against 33 girls for every 100 boys at all levels in 1950-51, their number increased to 55 in 1980-81. The enrolment of girls in all institutions and at all levels of education has gone up from 64 lakh in 1950-51 to 398.64 lakh in 1980-81 (Bhandari, 1982:33). But again we are to remember that there is a variation in enrolment by faculty. Then again, some of the trends are positive and significant in so far as they reflect major gains for women in education. However, these statistics also indicate certain negative trends. For instance, the percentage of females in total illiteracy has increased from 53.6 per cent in 1950-51 to 56.4 in 1980-81.[20]

The backwardness of Indian Muslims in literacy was clearly evident in the census of 1911. The census of 1911 stated that education, specially elementary education, began to spread among the Muslims in successive periods. The census of 1911 noted that the literacy rate of the Muslims was only about 5 per cent. According to the 1921 census, the Muslims had one literate male in every 11 males, i.e., 9 per cent, and one female in every 116 females, i.e., 0.86 per cent. In the 1931 census the literacy figures among the Muslims was 64 per 1,000, i.e., about 6.4 per cent (Mondal, 1997).

In general, the Muslims of India suffered much and the position of their women in every respect was the worst. Those who wanted to protect the woman and her interests by taking possession of her property, by putting her under lock and key, by whipping and flogging her, and by torturing her in various ways, did not think it proper to educate her and provide her with the opportunities to develop her mind, character and personality; rather they put all kinds of obstacles in her way to the fountain of knowledge. Sir Syed Ahmad Khan would be remembered for all times to come for his leadership in the field of modern education among the Indian Muslims. The educational movement started by Sir Syed and its philosophy put forward by Iqbal gave impetus to the origin and growth of educational institution for Muslim boys and girls in different parts of India by the end of the first decade of this century.[21] Speaking before the Education Commission in 1892, Sir Syed held four causes to be responsible for the educational backwardness of Indian Muslims---political traditions, social customs, religious beliefs and poverty; and these religious beliefs of Muslim society hindered the path of women's education.

The question that now arises is why women in India were left uneducated? Kailasbasini Devi[22] observes:

> According to all religious beliefs, whether Hinduism, Islam or Christianity, a wife is a man's better-half and is supposed to share half of his happiness or sorrows. But men, in actual practice, only gave them their share of sorrows, not happiness. Otherwise, why should they forbid education to their women? Actually they wanted to keep their women in perpetual slavery and were afraid of imparting education to them, which, as men feared, might elevate them to be man's equal.

Education in West Bengal has always been a guiding light for its inhabitants, a window to the world civilisation. The light, kindled by the Bengalis' aspiration for knowledge was upheld by educationists like Iswar Chandra Vidyasagar, Raja Rammohan Roy, Rabindranath Tagore and many other luminaries of the academic domain. But, strangely enough, they did nothing for education of Muslim women in undivided Bengal. Journalist Mujibar Rahaman,[23] in his presidential address to the All-Bengal Muslim Youth Conference which was held at Barddhaman in 1927, spoke out strongly against the patriarchal system's culpability in the continuing backwardness of Muslim society.

> It needs no reiteration in the twentieth century that the education of women is essential for the society. No development of the society is possible with half of the population remaining in the darkness of ignorance. The education of a child begins even when he/she sucks from the mother breast. So, please educate the women, help them to acquire knowledge. It is the selfishness of

> men that has kept the women away from education. Had this selfishness of men been prompted by high moral principles, the fate of women would have been different. That very selfishness would educate women to make them proper companions for men, the true producer of social good.

Here we can mention the name of Taharannessa and Rokeya Sakhawat Hossein who took the lead for education among Bengali Muslim women. Both of them realised that men alone could not bring about the desired change, women had a definitive role to play in family and society. But women were unable to do so because of their ignorance and backwardness. Rokeya[24] took the initiative and established a girls' school for Muslim women in West Bengal. She argues:

> The worst crime which our brothers commit against us is to deprive us of education. There is always some grandfather or elderly uncle who stands in the way of any poor girl who might wish to be educated. From experience we find that mothers are generally willing to educate their girls, but they are quite helpless when their husbands and other male relations will not hear of girls attending schools. May we challenge such grandfathers, fathers or uncles to show the authority on which they prevent their girls from acquiring education? Can they quote from the Holy *Quran* or *Hadis* any injunctions prohibiting women from obtaining knowledge.

Regarding the position of Bengali Muslim women's education, she has lamented that:

> It seems to me that even those Bengali-speaking Mohammedan families that are residing in Calcutta do not quite appreciate the advantage of school education for their girls. From the experience I have gained during these seven years I have noticed the Urdu-speaking people are more keen on sending their girls to school and that Bengali speaking families are less enterprising in this respect.

Here, we are to remember that the social structure could stimulate some change but it could also pose a few problems. Changes in the normative structure and organisational forms in society do not take place at the same time; the difference in their pace creates some problems. M. Indu Menon shows that reforms in law and educational policy do not always have the desired impact because of the normative and structural unpreparedness of Muslim society to accept their goals and means. As Lowie[25] put it in 1920:

> It is important to ascertain what customary or written-law and philosophical theory have to say on feminine rights and obligations. But, it is more important to know whether social practice conforms to theory or leaves it halting in the rear, as it so frequently does.

In this regard Vibhuti Patel[26] argues:

> During the last decade, women from different religious background have challenged the constitutional validity of the discriminatory aspect of personal laws, of laws that say that
>
> - a Hindu woman cannot have coparcenary rights over ancestral property,
> - a christian woman cannot obtain a divorce on her initiative, or
> - a muslim woman can be given oral divorce anytime, and so on and so forth.

She further states that:

> Lata Mittal challenged the Hindu Code Bill to compel her brother to let her live in the ancestral home. Mary Roy won equal inheritance rights for Syrian Christian women. Shahnaz Shaikh challenged the *Sharia* in the Supreme Court. Laru Janco of Singhbhoom and Bhuribai and Najubai Gamib of Dhulia filed a petition in the Supreme Court of India demanding land rights of tribal women. Hundreds of women filed petitions in lower courts

for divorce, maintenance, alimony, custody of children, etc. Most of them had to pay a heavy price for doing this because their families disowned them, and became hostile, some of them were even excommunicated by their community for questioning their 'cultural heritage' and 'customs' ....

This unpreparedness of Muslim society has been found in the case of Shah Banu judgment. Shah Bano Begum's case has stirred the Indian Muslims to an unprecedented degree.

The judgment aroused a great controversy. Delivered by a Constitution Bench of five judges, comprising Chief Justice Y.V. Chandrachud, Justice Chinappa Reddy and Justice Ranganath Misra, confirmed the right of Shah Banu Begum, a needy divorced Muslim woman, to maintenance. It awarded maintenance from her husband Ahmad Khan, an affluent advocate of Indore, beyond the customary period of three months—*iddat*, until her death or remarriage.

The Muslim fundamentalists in India have opposed the Supreme Court judgment granting the rights of maintenance to a divorced Muslim woman on the basis of their interpretation of Islamic laws. Denouncing the verdict, spokesman of different Muslim organisations such as Muslim Personal Law Board, Muslim Majlis Mushawarat, Jamat-e-Islami, Jamiat-ul-Ulema, Muslim League and others, declared that Islam was in danger. They all organised protest movements and agitations throughout India. Moulana Abdul Hasan Nadvi, President, Muslim Personal Law Board, compared the agitation with the Khilafat movement in the second decade of the twentieth century. To some extent the comparison stood valid. But the comparison is not totally valid in respect of the intent and consequences of the incident. Engineer[27] opines that the Khilafat agitation brought about Hindu-Muslim unity and strengthened the movement for Indian freedom. But this time, the Muslim agitation intended to divide the two communities and thus had a sectarian bias.

Then also, the question of economic activities of the divorced and separated Muslim women should be measured in accordance with their position in society. The dictate of the *Quran*[28] regarding this is as follows:

> He it is who made the earth even and smooth for you; so traverse through its sides, and eat of His provision. And unto Him will be the resurrection.

So we can argue that Islam grants to all the individuals equal rights to carry on any lawful occupation. But, peculiarly enough, in *Surah* 4, 34, the *Quran* utters:

> Men are the protectors and maintainers of women, because, *Allah* has given the one more (strength) than the other,, and because they support them from their means. Therefore, the righteous women are devoutly obedient, and guard in (the husband's) absence what *Allah* would have them guard. As to those women on whose part ye fear disloyalty and ill-conduct, admonish them (first), (next), refuse to share their beds, (and last) beat them (lightly); but if they return to obedience, seek not against them means (of annoyance): for Allah is Most High, Great (above you all).

It means *Allah* has made man superior to woman, and man has authority over woman because he spends his wealth to maintain her. This *Surah* of the *Quran* implies that, Islam has a equalitarian attitude towards all men, but the women are definitely in the lower rung of the status hierarchy. Man is the supporter and protector of woman in the family. Shibani Roy[29] observes:

> Thus, it is obvious that in a traditional Islamic set-up, a great deal of importance is attached to the man's role and his authoritarian position as a patriarch. Contrasted to the man's important role as the breadwinner for the entire household, the woman's roles are non-glamourous and have less importance attached to them, thus, resulting in her subordinate status in the family.

For a general understanding of the situation, we may conclude that the question of subjugation of Muslim women, in general, and divorced and separated Muslim women in West Bengal, in particular, have to be viewed from the larger sociological point of view. Qurratulain Hyder[30], while discussing the situation of the Muslim women, says that they are as modern and as backward as their counterparts in the various income groups in other communities. The various economic and sociological problems of the Muslim community cannot be isolated from the problem of general backwardness and poverty of the Indian masses.

Any betterment of the status of the divorced and separated Muslim women in West Bengal demands positive attacks on poverty, illiteracy and on social restrictions which presuppose male superiority and dominance. Women's economic independence is an important factor for the liberation and betterment of women's status. Regarding this Engels[31] observes:

> Emancipation of women becomes possible only when women are enabled to take part in production on a large social scale and when domestic duties require attention only to a minor degree. And this has become possible only as a result of modern large-scale industries, which not only permit the participation of women in production in large numbers, but actually call for it and, moreover, strive to convert private domestic work also into public industry.

Notes

1. Government of India (1975): *Report of the Committee on the Status of Women in India*, New Delhi: Department of Social Welfare, p. vii.

2. Imtiaz Ahmad (ed.) (1976): *Family, Kinship and Marriage among Muslims in India*, New Delhi: Manohar, p. xviii.
3. Raunaq Jahan: Quoted by M.Y. Siddiqui (1987): *Muslim Women in Transition: A Social Profile*, New Delhi: Harnam Publication, p.1.
4. Imtiaz Ahmad (ed.) (1973): *Caste and Social Stratification among the Muslims*, Delhi: Manohar, p. vii.
5. S. Musi Raza: Quoted by Talat Ara Ashrafi (1992): *Muslim Women in the Changing Perspective*, New Delhi: Commonwealth Publishers, p. 34.
6. M. Indu Menon (1981): *Status of Muslim Women in India*, New Delhi: Uppal Publishing House. p. vii.
7. M.Y. Siddiqui (1987): Ibid, p.1.
8. Andre Beteille: "The Position of Women in Indian Society" in Devaki Jain (ed.) (1976): *Indian Women*, New Delhi: Publication Divisions, Government of India, p. 61.
9. Shibani Roy (1979): *Status of Muslim Women in India*, Delhi: B.R. Publishing Corporation.
10. Ibid, p.21.
11. Ibid, p.37.
12. Ibid, p.45.
13. M. Indu Menon: op. cit.
14. Talat Ara Ashrafi (1992): op. cit.
15. Rafiuddin Ahmad (1981): *The Bengal Muslims 1871-1906: A Quest for Identity*, Delhi: Oxford University Press.
16. Ranjit K. Bhattacharya (1991): *Moslems of Rural Bengal*, Calcutta: Subarnaekha.
17. M.K.A. Siddiqui (1974): *Muslims of Calcutta*, Calcutta: Anthropological Survey of India.
18. Zarina Bhatty: "Status of Muslim Women and Social Change" in B.R. Nanda (ed.) (1976): *Indian Women from Purdah to Modernity*, New Delhi: Vikas Publishing House Pvt. Ltd.
19. Imtiaz Ahmad (1976): op. cit., p. xx.

20. Karuna Chanana (ed.) (1988): *Socialization Education and Women*, New Delhi: Orient Longman, p.1.
21. Jamila Brijbhushan (1980): *Muslim Women in Pardah and Out of it*, New Delhi: Vikas Publishing House Pvt. Ltd.
22. Kailasbasini Devi (1865): *Hindu Abalakuler Bidyabhyas O Tahar Sammunnati* (in Bengali), Calcutta, pp. 11-12.
23. Mujibar Rahaman (1927): Quoted by Dr. Laila Zaman (ed.): *The Mussalman Patrikai Rokeya Proshanga* (in Bengali), Dhaka: Bangla Academy, p. 13.
24. Dr. Laila Zaman (ed.) (1994): Ibid p.24.
25. Quoted by Shibani Roy (1979): Op. cit., p.1.
26. Vibhuti Patel: "The Shah Bano Controversy and the Challenges Faced by Women's Movement in India" in Asghar Ali Engineer (ed.) (1995): *Problems of Muslim Women in India*, Bombay: Orient Longman. pp. 140-141.
27. Asghar Ali Engineer (ed.) (1987): *The Shah Bano Controversy*, Bombay: Orient Longman.
28. The *Quran*: Surah 67: 15.
29. Shibani Roy: op. cit., p.92.
30. Qurratulain Hyder: "Muslim Women in India" in Devaki Jain (ed.): op. cit., p. 201.
31. F. Engels (1973): *Origin of Family, Private Property and State*, Moscow: Selected Works. Vol. 3, p. 32.

2

Survey and Methodology

The main focus of the study is to depict the present position of the divorced and separated Muslim women belonging to two *gram panchayats* in two districts of West Bengal and thereby we also try to trace out the operation of the system of divorce and the factors responsible for such practices. The thrust of the present study is, however, empirical, seeking to find out (a) the nature and magnitude of the problem, (b) how it operates, (c) the social and other causes due to which the practice of divorce and separation among Bengali muslim women persists, (d) variation between textual model and operational model about divorce and separation of Bengali Muslim women, and (e) the real position of Bengali Muslim women in the society.

For gaining an understanding of the problem it is imperative to analyse at first the nature of the two categories of the population.

'Divorced' Muslim women are those whose *talaq* or release from marriage has occurred in the presence of legal authorities or local elderly people. Here legal authorities mean *maulana, maulvi, imam*, while local elderly people mean those who have their authority for witnessing such action. It also includes those cases in which release from the marriage tie has occurred in the court.

On the other hand, 'separated' Muslim women are those who at present are living with their parents and do not have any connection with their husbands. These women, however, may harbour the fond hope that their husbands would one day give due recognition to them and take them back with honour.

To carry out this study, it was necessary to specify and identify areas of investigation on which information was needed and also the method through which this information was to be collected. Since there was no previous research in this particular field, the present survey is essentially a descriptive one which would accurately portray the characteristics of the divorced and separated Muslim women in West Bengal. By descriptive study we can test some initial hypotheses and provide initial information for further research in this field, rather than finally test and examine previously established theories.

To understand the problem more precisely and accurately the researcher initially raised the following questions:

1. Is divorce widely practised among the Muslims? Is it correlated with their socio-economic status?
2. To what extent do religious prescription and practice vary with regard to *Sharia*?
3. Does the custom of *purdah* hamper or constrict the possibility of women's self-advancement through education and employment?
4. Are the rules of marriage and divorce especially restrictive for Muslim women? How do these restrict their social mobility and economic independence?
5. Does the minority status of Muslims reinforce the aspects of tradition or customary practices within the community?

To secure some guidelines, directions and suggestions for formulating the hypotheses of the research and its appropriate design, a pilot survey among 20 divorced/separated Bengali Muslim women in Mongolkote village in the district of Barddhaman, West Bengal was undertaken. To design is to plan; that is, designing is the process of making decisions before the situation arises in which the decision has to be carried out. It is, thus, a process of deliberate anticipation directed toward bringing an expected situation under control. In making a choice of procedure the researcher was guided by Sclltiz *et al*[1], who observe:

> A research design is the arrangement of conditions for collection and analysis of data in a manner that aims at combining relevance to the research purpose with economy in procedure.

On the basis of the experiences gained in the pilot survey, specific questions were selected for a more systematic study. After the completion of the pilot survey, the pattern of the study was finalised.

The first attempt in these trial interviews was to determine the problem of divorce and separation as perceived by the women themselves. The interviews were relatively unstructured and the question were open-ended. Notes were taken during the discussions at the time of conducting the pilot survey, and thus materials for formulating the hypotheses were collected.

During the period of the pilot survey, it was found that some questions were not clear to the respondents, and hence, had to be dropped during the later, detailed questioning. This also prompted greater care and caution in formulating the final questionnaire.

The present study being a descriptive one where the major emphasis was on the discovery of reasons behind divorce and separation in West Bengal, it was necessary that the research design must be flexible enough to permit the consideration of diverse aspects of the phenomenon. Hence, to gather as much information as possible and to make the study 'intensive', both the methods---interviews and case studies---were adopted for data collection. Two different interview schedules were prepared for divorced and separated Bengali Muslim women and the heads of the families for collecting information pertaining to the study. Interview schedules contained questions on age, sex, caste like status, socio-economic condition of the divorced/separated Bengali Muslim women and their guardians, etc.

The Bengali version of the interview schedule greatly helped the researcher in collecting the information and data correctly. This way the problem of communication with the respondents was overcome.

As the study is 'descriptive' one, not much stress was laid on standardised answers such as 'yes', 'no', 'strongly agree' or to structured and routine questions. Also, it was not possible to foresee and hypothesise beforehand all the possible directions of the phenomenon, or to gauge which of the information collected would be useful to, and utilised for, the ultimate purpose of proper understanding. Hence, additional and supplementary information was collected through case studies, a technique which was very useful when it functioned as a supplementary to interview schedules.

Experience in the field survey revealed that first, a considerable degree of rapport with respondents was necessary. The right attitude and sentiments were needed as well as where intimate, delicate, complex, emotional and personal information was sought. This procedure was required so that the respondents could be adequately persuaded to be candid in answering questions and narrating their experiences. In-depth interviews provided a very useful method for achieving this end. If the respondent was allowed to follow his/her own train of thought, answers to many questions could be obtained automatically. And, for these reasons, some amount of time had to be spent with a respondent to establish a kind of relationship. Once rapport had been established, irrelevant conversation was stopped without the awareness of the respondent, leaving her confident and at ease facilitating exchange of information. Though this was a time-consuming method, yet it appeared to be suitable and applicable for the present purpose.

G.B. Allport,[2] in his classic statement, sums this up brilliantly in the following way:

> If you want to know how people feel, what they experience and what they remember, what their emotions and motives are like, and the reasons for acting as they do why not ask them?

This direct interview method with a interview schedule helped the researcher in a variety of ways. By this method, an interviewer is supposed to observe not only what the respondent says verbally, but also how he/she says it, and by this way, can appraise the validity of what the respondent says, or can even cross-check his/her statement if so required.

However, the researcher is not asserting the relative efficiency, or rather, significance of any particular technique of data collection. The researcher is only stating his own field experiences and the justification for the techniques used for the study.

Once the problem to be tackled in the course of research was finally settled, the researcher proceeded to formulate tentative solutions. These proposed solutions or explanations constituted the hypotheses which were to be tested on the basis of facts already known or those that can be made known.

In this regard Lundberg[3] remarks:

> The only difference between gathering data without a hypothesis and gathering them with one is that in the latter case, we deliberately recognize the limitations of our senses and attempt to reduce their fallibility by limiting our field of investigation so as to prevent greater concentration of attention on particular aspects which past experience leads us to believe are insignificant for our purpose.

So we may argue that a hypothesis helps us to see and appreciate the kind of data that must be collected from the field in order to answer our research questions and also the way in which they should be organised most efficiently.

Webster's New International Dictionary of English language, 1956, defines the word 'hypothesis' as:

> ...a proposition, condition or principle which is assumed, perhaps without belief, in order to draw out its logical consequences and by this method to test its accord with facts which are known or may be determined.

The researcher also formulated a tentative solution of the problem. This way, it is anticipated that certain logical consequences would be observed on the plane of observable events or objects. The hypotheses of the present study are as follows:

---- Divorce among Muslim women is more prevalent among the low-income groups and low-status groups.

---- There is a wide divergence between theory and practice in respect of marriage and divorce among the Muslims.

---- Divorced/separated Muslim women do not play any crucial role in the family's decision-making process.

---- The custom of *purdah* is widely prevalent among the divorced/separated Muslim women in West Bengal.

---- Seclusion and lack of education create in divorced/separated Muslim women a low level of aspiration and this, in turn, dissuades them from striving for status mobility.

---- The traditional value system of Muslim society assigns to the woman a position subordinate to man and this value system is still in operation in Muslim society.

According to the 1991 census, the total Muslim population in West Bengal was 1,60,75,836; of which 83,60,835 were males and 77,15,001 were females. They constituted 23.61 per cent of the total population in the state. Though Muslims live all over West Bengal, the proportion of Muslims in rural areas is higher

(1,35,45,929, i.e., 84.26%) than that of the urban areas (25,29,907 i.e., 15.74%). The Muslims are mainly concentrated in rural areas owing to their ties with the land. The districts in which the proportion of Muslims exceeds the state average of 23.61 per cent are Murshidabad (61.40%), Maldah (47.49%), West Dinajpur (36.75%), Birbhum (33.06%), 24 Parganas (N) (24.17%), 24 Parganas (S) (29.24%), and Nadia (24.92%). The districts in which the Muslims constitute 20 per cent or more, but less than the state average 23.61 per cent are Kooch Bihar (23.34%), Howrah (22.22%). The remaining districts with less than 10% or more but less than state average are Calcutta (17.72%), Barddhaman (19.55%), Hoogly (14.52%), Jalpaiguri (10.74%), Medinipur (10.78%), Bankura (6.63%), Purulia (5.98%) and Darjeeling (4.55%) (see Table 2.1).

Table 2.1

Growth of Muslim Population in West Bengal, 1971-81

State/District	*Census Year*	*Population*	*Percentage to Total Population*	*Percentage Increase 1971-81 and 1981-91*
West Bengal	1991	1,60,75,836	23.61	36.89
	1981	1,17,43,209	21.51	29.55
	1971	90,64,338	20.46	—
Kooch Bihar	1991	5,06,728	23.34	37.63
	1981	3,68,176	20.78	22.52.
	1971	3,00,496	21.25	—
Jalpaiguri	1991	2,81,054	10.04	45.13
	1981	1,93,658	8.75	23.36
	1971	1,56,992	8.97	—
Darjeeling	1991	59,140	4.55	58.55
	1981	37,299	3.64	58.56
	1971	23,523	3.01	—
West Dinajpur	1991	11,49,560	36.75	33.55
	1981	8,60,797	35.79	28.95
	1971	6,67,547	35.89	—

Contd...

Contd...

Maldah	1991	12,52,292	47.49	36.13
	1981	9,19,918	45.27	32.27
	1871	6,95,504	43.13	—
Murshidabad	1991	29,10,220	61.40	34.16
	1981	21,69,121	58.67	30.67
	1971	16,59,988	56.34	—
24 Parganas	1991	34,71,136	21.59	35.39
	1981	25,63,751	24.08	37.51
	1971	20,00,844	23.34	—
Nadia	1991	9,59,998	24.92	34.49
	1981	7,13,776	23.87	28.13
	1971	5,19,086	23.68	—
Calcutta	1991	7,79,433	17.72	53.75
	1981	5,06,942	15.34	13.43
	1971	4,46,932	14.20	—
Howrah	1991	8,28,740	22.22	38.48
	1981	5,98,448	20.17	37.17
	1971	4,35,199	18.00	—
Hoogly	1991	6,32,175	14.52	29.15
	1981	4,89,494	13.76	32.17
	1971	3,70,354	12.89	—
Medinipur	1991	8,98,478	10.78	53.17
	1981	5,86,587	8.70	37.55
	1971	4,26,463	7.74	—
Bankura	1991	1,86,021	6.63	38.73
	1981	1,34,085	5.45	36.14
	1971	98,489	4.85	—
Purulia	1991	1,33,119	5.98	31.79
	1981	1,01,044	5.45	35.79
	1971	74,410	4.64	—
Barddhaman	1991	11,82,755	19.55	38.99
	1981	8,50,951	17.60	26.59
	1971	6,72,277	17.17	—
Birbhum	1991	8,44,987	33.06	30.15
	1981	6,49,212	30.98	25.24
	1971	5,18,381	29.19	—

Source: Census of India 1991.

In Table 2.1 we find that Muslims live all over West Bengal. There are certain districts like Murshidabad, Maldah, West Dinajpur which have larger concentration of Muslim population than other districts, whereas districts like Bankura and Purulia have smaller concentration of Muslim population. The district of Murshidabad accounts for 61.40 per cent and Barddhaman 19.55 per cent of the total Muslim population in West Bengal, while the proportion of Muslim population in the state is 23.61 per cent (see Table 2.1). Accordingly, these two districts were chosen for data collection. Two *gram panchayats* were selected, i.e., Mongolkote *gram panchayat* and Panchathupi *gram panchayat* from Barddhaman and Murshidabad districts respectively. Mongolkote *gram panchayat* is within the jurisdiction of Mongolkote police station and Panchthupi *gram panchayat* falls within the jurisdiction of Burwan police station.

The main reason behind selecting these two *gram panchayats* is that since our objective is to study the present position of the divorced and separated Muslim women in West Bengal and the variation of the textual and operational models of their plight, it was attempted to select areas which can be treated as representative of the entire West Bengal population. Now, the Bengali Muslim population is mainly clustered in rural areas, as revealed by the demographic statistics. Nearly 84.26 per cent of the total Muslim population is living in rural areas (see Table 2.2). On the other hand, the Bengali rural Muslim population is mainly engaged in agricultural and allied activities. In Murshidabad, 94.18 per cent and in Barddhaman 77.29 per cent are living in rural areas—48.63 per cent females in Murshidabad district live in rural areas and 48.32 per cent in Barddhaman district. It was, therefore, sought to focus attention on areas which broadly conformed to the above characteristics, viz., rural setting and an agrarian economic setup. Both Panchathupi and Mongolkote *gram panchayats* of Barddhaman and Murshidabad districts perfectly fitted the requirements, as the area of survey reveals typical rural characteristics. Also, the researcher's familiarity with the localities and people prompted him to select these two areas. As there was no secondary data on divorced/separated Muslim women in West Bengal, the researcher has taken the census of these two categories of people living in Mongolkote *gram panchayat* and Panchthupi *gram panchayat* of Barddhaman and Murshidabad districts, respectively. Consequently, there is no chance of omission of any rich or middle-class divorced/separated Muslim women. Guardians like father, mother, brother, etc., of the divorced and separated Muslim women have also been interviewed.

Table 2.2
Percentages Showing Household Population by Religion of Head of the Household

State/District/ Police Station	*Households*	*Muslims*		
		Persons	*Males*	*Females*
West Bengal				
Rural	72.52	84.26	51.36	48.64
Urban	27.48	15.74	55.48	44.52
Barddhaman				
Rural	64.91	77.30	51.68	48.32
Urban	35.09	22.70	54.98	45.02
Mongolkote P.S.				
Rural	100	100	100	100
Urban	—	—	—	—
Murshidabad				
Rural	89.57	94.18	51.37	48.63
Urban	10.43	5.82	50.78	49.22
Burwan P.S.				
Rural	100	100	100	100
Urban	—	—	—	—

Source: Census of India 1991.

Table 2.3

Number and Percentages of Villages and Rural Population

State/ District		*Inhabited Villages*	*Rural Population*		
			Persons	*Males*	*Females*
West Bengal	n	37,910	4,93,70,364	2,54,42,210	2,39,28,154
	%	100	100	100	100
Barddhaman	n	2,488	39,27,613	20,31,842	18,95,771
	%	6.56	7.96	7.99	7.92
Murshidabad	n	1,918	42,45,802	21,86,950	20,58,852
	%	5.06	8.60	8.59	8.60

Source: Census India 1991.

In Table 2.3 we find that rural population in West Bengal was 4,93,70,364; among which 2,54,42,210 were males and 2,39,28,154 were females. Corresponding figure for Barddhaman was 39,27,613, i.e., 7.56 per cent of total West Bengal population of which 7.99 per cent were males and 7.92 per cent were females. In Murshidabad we find that total rural population was 42,45,802, i.e., 8.60 per cent of which 21,86,950, i.e., 8.59 per cent were males and 20,58,852, i.e., 8.60 per cent were females.

If we go through Table 2.4, we observe that the condition of Bengali women is very poor. According to 1991 census, divorce and separation more evident in rural areas than urban areas. It is interesting to note that in the divorced/separated category (see Table 2.4) females outnumbered the males. The females percentage of divorce and separation was 83.92 per cent in rural West Bengal; 76.43 per cent in Barddhaman and 91.40 per cent in Murshidabad.

Table 2.4
Percentage of Population: Sex and Marital Statuswise

State/ District	Total Population		Married		Divorced/Separated	
	Males	Females	Males	Females	Males	Females
West Bengal						
Rural	71.65	73.47	69.69	72.49	77.99	83.92
Urban	28.35	26.53	30.31	27.51	22.01	16.08
Barddhaman						
Rural	63.76	66.20	63.02	65.71	61.89	76.43
Urban	36.24	33.80	36.98	34.29	38.11	23.57
Murshidabad						
Rural	89.65	89.48	89.49	89.66	92.20	91.40
Urban	10.35	10.52	10.51	10.34	7.80	8.60

Source: Census of India 1991.

Classification of the Respondents

In the district of Barddhaman, the Mongolkote *gram panchayat* includes the following villages: Mongolkote, Baxinagar, Aral, Kamalpur, Jaharpur, Deulia, Mahartuba-Khurtuba, Barobazar, Nutunhat and Puratanhat. In some of the villages there is no Muslim Population at all. Seventy divorced/separated Muslim women were interviewed in Mongolkote *gram panchayat* among whom 31 respondents were divorcees and 39 separated (see Table 2.5), 52 guardians were also interviewed in Mongolkote *gram panchayat*. Among these, 16 respondents were fathers, 28 mothers, seven brothers and one elder sister, while the remaining 19 women had no guardians (see Table 2.6).

In the district of Murshidabad, the Panchthupi *gram panchayat* was identified which includes the following villages: Panchthupi, Godapara, Pulia, Muniadi, Belgram and Achuapara. Here 58 respondents were interviewed among whom 36 respondents were divorcees and 22 were separated. Forty-seven guardians were also interviewed among which 17 respondents were fathers, 27 mothers, 3 brothers and 11 women had no guardians at all (see Table 2.6). The justification for interviewing the guardians was that as heads of the family they control all channels of communication. It is useful to know how they rationalise their actions even though some of these actions are at variance with the injunctions of great traditions of Islam.

Table 2.5

Gram Panchayats and Number of Respondents

Gram Panchayats	*Divorced*	*Separated*	*Total*
Mongolkote	31	39	70
Panchthupi	36	22	58
Total	67	61	128

Table 2.6

Gram Panchayats and Number of Guardians

Guardians	*Mongolkote*	*Panchthupi*	*Total*
Fathers	16	17	33
Mothers	28	27	55
Brothers	07	03	10
Elder sister	01	00	01
No guardians	18	11	29
Total	70	58	128

In aggregate, 67 divorced and 61 separated Muslim women belonging to the two *gram panchayats* in two districts of West Bengal were interviewed. We also interviewed the guardians for their opinions, among which 33 were fathers, 55 mothers, 10 brothers, one elder sister and the remaining 29 respondents had no guardians at all (see Table 2.6).

The field studies relating to this research were mainly conducted in the month of May-June 1990 in Mongolkote *gram panchayat* of Barddhaman district and September-October 1990 in Panchathupi *gram panchayat* of Murshidabad district. The researcher further visited the localities in the month of October 1992 for some additional information.

Belonging as he did to the same religion as the respondent, the researcher faced no major problem in establishing rapport with the villagers. But some of the respondents were rather confused about the purpose of the researcher's visit. The researcher categorically told them that he was not a government man and the data collected was to be used strictly for academic purposes. Only in one village in Murshidabad district, villagers did not allow the researcher to talk with the respondents.

In a few cases, establishing rapport was a problem and the members of the family of the divorced/separated women suspected the researcher to be an agent of the husband and at first would not even let him in. In some cases, the interview was taken with permission from other members of the family. There was no problem with interviewing guardians.

Usually, the interviews lasted for 40 to 50 minutes in each case depending on the time required to gain rapport.

Notes

1. Johada Sclltiz *et al* (1969): *Research Methods in Social Relations*, Methuen and Co. Ltd., p. 31.
2. G.B. Allport: Quoted by Selltiz *et al*, Ibid, p. 236.
3. G.A. Lundberg (1926): *Social Research*, New York: Longmans Green and Company, p. 119.

3

Muslim Communities in Contemporary India

Any attempt to study the divorced and separated Muslim women in West Bengal should be viewed from a larger social framework because its structure, cultural norms and value judgements are important determinants of the community. Social traditions and practices play a vital influence in shaping the attitudes as well as behaviour patterns of human groups and communities. Hence, emerging trends of society cannot be viewed in isolation from them. For an understanding of the problem of the divorced and separated Muslim women in West Bengal it is imperative to consider the demographic statistics of Muslims in the country.

According to the 1991 census, the Muslim population in India is 10,15,96,057, of which 5,26,31,365 are males and 4,89,64,692 are females. But we are to remember that the Muslims in India are not a homogenous community. They have their differences on the question of language, culture, behavioural pattern, etc. Given this character of the Muslim population the question arises—is there anything like a 'Muslim problem'? This and other related questions are being asked today and discussed, but there is little awareness, and what is more, no viable answer to them seems to be possible unless we bear in our mind the social structure of the Muslim community in India which has set the pattern. As a community, it is an integral part of the Indian society, irrespective of the fact that today it is confronted with certain particular problems that are as much a consequence of its historical role as the product of its own social attitude.

Muslims are scattered all over India, from a high concentration of 64.19 per cent of the total population in Jammu and Kashmir (1981 census) to a low density of 1.82 per cent in Orissa (1991 census). (see Tables 3.3 and 3.4). The Muslims constitute a high percentage of the total Indian population in the following states (see Table 3.1).

Table 3.1

Highly Muslim Concentrated States in India
(10 per cent and above of the total population)

*Name of the State**	*Percentage of the Total Population*			
	1961	*1971*	*1981*	*1991*
Jammu and Kashmir	68.30	65.85	64.19	-
Assam	23.29	24.03	-	28.43
West Bengal	20.00	20.46	21.51	23.61
Kerala	17.90	19.50	21.25	23.33
Uttar Pradesh	14.63	15.48	15.93	17.33
Bihar	12.45	13.48	14.13	14.81

Source: Census of India 1991—Religion.

* No Census was conducted in Assam and Jammu & Kashmir in 1981 and 1991 respectively.

Moreover, in some districts of all these states over 30 per cent of the total population are Muslims.

Table 3.2
Highly Muslim Concentrated Districts in India (over 30% of the total population)

State	*District*	*Percentage of the Total Muslim Population*	*Percentage of Total Muslim Population*	
			Rural	*Urban*
	Goalpara	50.18	92.57	7.49
Assam	Nowgong	47.19	96.41	3.59
	Cachar	63.42	86.51	13.49
Bihar	Purnea	34.53	95.25	4.75
Kerala	Kozhikode	36.23	59.01	40.99
	Murshidabad	61.40	94.18	5.82
West Bengal	Maldah	47.49	98.31	1.69
	West Dinajpur	36.35	98.30	1.70
	Rampur	47.95	62.72	37.28
Uttar Pradesh	Moradabad	42.69	61.47	38.53
	Bijnor	40.35	59.32	40.68
	Saharanpur	36.12	67.18	32.82

Source: Census of India 1991—Religion.

From an analysis of Table 3.2 we can infer that Muslims in India are mainly concentrated in rural areas. But in Uttar Pradesh there are some urban concentrations of Muslim population. In Rampur and Moradabad districts the concentrations of Muslim population in urban areas are 37.28 per cent and 38.53 per cent, respectively. But in the 1971 census, it was found that 27 per cent of the total Muslim population lives in urban areas. Further, whereas in the high percentage (over 10%) Muslim populated states, the main concentration is in rural areas, in the low percentage states (below 10%) urban Muslims constitute a sizeable proportion of the total Muslim population.

Table 3.3

High Muslim Concentration in Rural Areas of India

States	*Percentage of the Total Muslim Population*	*Percentage of Total Muslim Population*	
		Rural	*Urban*
Assam	28.43	94.71	5.29
West Bengal	23.61	84.26	15.74
Kerala	23.33	73.43	26.57
Uttar Pradesh	17.33	64.35	35.65
Bihar	14.80	84.43	15.57
Punjab	1.18	60.50	39.50
Haryana	4.64	90.07	9.93

Source: Census of India 1991—Religion.

Table 3.4

High Muslim Concentration in Urban Areas of India

State	*Percentage of the Total Muslim Population*	*Percentage of Total Muslim Population*	
		Rural	*Urban*
Andhra Pradesh	8.91	41.83	58.17
Gujarat	8.73	41.53	58.47
Madhya Pradesh	4.96	36.13	63.87
Tamil Nadu	6.54	30.91	69.19
Maharashtra	9.66	33.05	66.95
Mysore	11.64	44.50	55.50
Rajasthan	8.01	50.77	49.23
Orissa	1.82	60.73	39.27

Source: Census of India 1991—Religion.

Table 3.5
Muslim Population in Industrial Districts of West Bengal and Bihar

State	*District*	*Percentage of the Total Muslim Population*	*Percentage of the Total Muslim Population*	
			Rural	*Urban*
West Bengal	Calcutta	17.72	-	100.00
	Barddhaman	19.55	77.29	22.71
	Howrah	22.22	54.64	45.36
	Dhanbad	12.33	69.37	30.63
Bihar	Hazaribagh	13.17	78.59	21.41
	Ranchi	10.35	47.53	52.47
	Singhbum	8.09	7.82	92.18

Source: Census of India 1991—Religion.

Table 3.6
Muslim Population in Agricultural Districts of West Bengal and Bihar

State	*District*	*Muslim Percentage of Total Population*	*Percentage of the Total Muslim Population*	
			Rural	*Urban*
West Bengal	Murshidabad	61.40	94.18	5.82
	Maldah	47.49	98.31	1.69
	West Dinajpur	36.75	98.30	1.70
	Nadia	24.92	96.07	3.93
	Purnea	34.83	95.25	4.75
Bihar	Saharsa	14.48	90.55	9.45
	Dharbhanga	22.12	89.34	10.66
	Purba Champaran	18.41	91.39	8.61
	Paschim Champaran	20.58	87.93	12.07

Source: Census of India 1991—Religion.

A comparatively high concentration of the Muslim population in urban areas is noticeable in the states that have either developed or have emerged because of rapid economic developments and a high rate of economic growth (see Table 3.4). Whereas in areas which grew before independence, Muslims are still concentrated in rural areas. Both the patterns clearly indicate that Muslims are much more urbanized in those states where process of urbanization is newer and faster (i.e. northwestern, western and southern regions) than in others (i.e., eastern and north-eastern regions).

Table 3.7

High Muslim-Concentrated Districts of West Bengal with Percentage Increase during 1971-81 and 1981-91

District	*Percentage of the Total Muslim Population*			*Percentage Increase of Muslim Population (1971-81)*	*Percentage Increase of Muslim Population (1981-91)*
	1991	*1981*	*1971*		
Murshidabad	61.40	58.67	56.34	30.67	34.16
Maldah	47.49	45.27	43.13	32.27	36.13
West Dinajpur	36.75	35.79	35.89	29.71	33.55

Source: Census of India 1991—Religion.

Under this general pattern of Muslims in India, we are to analyze the general pattern of Muslims in West Bengal. According to the 1991 census, the total Muslim population in West Bengal was 1,60,75,836 among which 83,60,835 were males and 77,15,001 were females. But in 1981 census the total Muslim population in West Bengal was 1,17,43,259 of which 61,00,517 were males and 56,42,742 were females. It means the percentage of Muslim population in West Bengal had increased from 21.51 per cent in 1981 to 23.61 per cent in 1991. It was noted that in West Bengal, the proportion of Muslims in rural areas was higher---84.26 per cent---than that of urban population---15.74 per cent (see Table 3.3). This is due to their traditional ties with the land. It is also found that the migration of rural Muslims to urban areas of Calcutta and other district towns was not very high during the preceding years.

According to 1991 census, Murshidabad is the only district in West Bengal where Muslims are the majority in number, comprising 61.40 per cent of the total population against 38.60 per cent of non-Muslims, particularly Hindus. Murshidabad, thus, emerges as the only district with a Muslim majority except for Kashmir in the mainland India. Other districts which have 30 per cent and above Muslims are Maldah (47.49%) and West Dinajpur (36.75%) respectively. But in Darjeeling Muslims are the least in number (4.55%).

Table 3.8

High Muslim-Concentration in Rural Areas of West Bengal

Districts	*Percentage of the Total Muslim Population*	*Percentage of Muslim Population*	
		Rural	*Urban*
Jalpaiguri	10.04	93.55	6.45
Kooch Bihar	23.34	97.43	2.57
West Dinajpur	36.75	98.30	1.70
Maldah	47.49	98.31	1.69
Murshidabad	61.40	94.18	5.82
Nadia	24.92	96.07	3.93
Birbhum	33.06	94.84	5.16
Bankura	6.63	94.27	5.73
Medinipur	10.78	90.42	9.58

Source: Census of India 1991—Religion.

If we go through Table 3.8 and Table 3.9, then we find that in agriculture-based districts the Muslims are mainly concentrated in rural areas. As for example we can cite the case of the following districts: Jalpaiguri, Kooch Bihar, West Dinajpur, Maldah, Murshidabad, Nadia, Birbhum, Bankura and Medinipur. It is also to be noticed that rural concentration is clearly evident in north Bengal districts except Darjeeling. Though the Muslims are smaller in number in Darjeeling and Purulia, they have 29.82 per cent and 11.79 per cent respectively urban concentration of Muslim population. Other than Calcutta, the highest urban concentration is to be found in Howrah (i.e., 22.22%).

Table 3.9

High Muslim Concentration in Urban Areas of West Bengal (more than 10% of total muslim population)

District	*Percentage of the Muslim Population*	*Percentage of Muslim Population*	
		Rural	*Urban*
Darjeeling	4.55	70.18	29.82
24 Parganas (N)	24.17	81.70	18.30
24 Parganas (S)	29.94	88.75	11.25
Howrah	22.22	54.64	45.35
Calcutta	17.72		100.00
Hoogly	14.52	78.05	21.95
Barddhaman	19.55	77.29	22.71
Purulia	5.98	88.21	11.79

Source: Census of India 1991—Religion.

According to 1991 census, in one district of West Bengal Muslims account for one-third of the total population, (i.e., West Dinajpur, 36.75%). Then the descending order follows: Birbhum (33.06%), Nadia (24.92%), 24 Parganas (N) (24.17%), 24 Parganas (S) (29.94%), Kooch Bihar (23.34%) and Howrah (22.22%).

It is also to be noted here that three south-west districts, namely, Purulia, Bankura and Medinipur have the highest percentage of the Hindus among their population. According to

1991 census, the followers of Islam in these three districts account for 5.98 per cent, 6.63 per cent and 10.78 per cent, respectively.

Table 3.10

Percentage of Muslim Male/Female Concentration in West Bengal

District	*Muslim Population as a Percentage of Total Population*	*Percentage of Total Muslim Population*		*Percentage of Total Rural Muslim Population*		*Percentage of Total Urban Muslim Population*	
		Males (%)	*Females (%)*	*Males (%)*	*Females (%)*	*Males (%)*	*Females (%)*
West Bengal	23.61	52.61	47.99	51.36	48.64	55.48	44.52
Darjeeling	4.55	54.70	45.30	52.75	47.25	59.28	40.72
Jalpaiguri	10.04	51.97	48.03	51.86	48.14	53.49	46.11
Kooch Bihar	23.34	51.46	48.54	51.45	48.55	51.85	48.15
West Dinajpur	36.75	51.57	48.43	51.49	48.51	55.90	44.10
Maldah	47.49	51.42	48.58	51.40	48.60	52.34	47.66
Murshidabad	61.40	51.33	48.67	51.37	48.63	50.78	49.22
Nadia	24.92	51.67	48.33	51.69	48.31	51.36	48.64
24 Parganas (N)	24.17	51.98	48.02	50.94	49.06	56.59	43.41
24 Parganas (S)	29.94	51.37	48.63	51.15	48.85	53.11	46.89
Howrah	22.22	52.86	47.14	51.73	48.27	54.21	45.79
Calcutta	17.72	58.13	41.87	-	-	58.13	41.87
Hoogly	14.52	52.10	47.90	50.90	49.10	56.34	43.66
Barddhaman	19.55	52.43	47.57	51.68	48.32	54.98	45.02
Birbhum	33.06	51.28	48.72	51.24	48.76	52.18	47.82
Bankura	6.63	51.80	48.20	51.66	48.34	54.21	45.79
Medinipur	10.78	51.42	48.58	51.29	48.71	52.71	47.29
Purulia	5.98	51.78	48.22	51.65	48.35	52.76	47.24

Source: Census of India 1991—Religion.

It is only in West Bengal that the real rural character of the Muslim population can be identified most clearly. In fact, the Bengali Muslims compare unfavourably with their national and regional counterparts on levels of urbanism. The national aver-

Table 3.11

Growth of Muslim Population in West Bengal During 1971-81 (30 Percent and Above Increase of Muslim Population with Percentage Increase among Hindus)

State/District	*Census Year*	*Percentage to Total Muslim Population*	*Percentage Increase*	
			Muslims	*Hindus*
West Bengal	1991	23.61	36.89	21.09
	1981	21.51	29.55	21.37
	1971	20.46	-	-
Darjeeling	1991	4.55	58.55	24.54
	1981	3.64	58.56	27.78
	1971	3.01	-	-
Medinipur	1991	10.78	53.17	19.79
	1981	8.70	37.55	20.90
	1971	7.74	-	-
24 Pargana* (N)	1991	24.17		
(S)	1991	29.94	35.39	16.50
	1981	24.08	37.51	32.5
	1971	23.34	-	-
Howrah	1991	22.22	38.48	22.48
	1981	20.17	37.17	19.28
	1971	18.00	-	-
Bankura	1991	6.63	38.73	14.54
	1981	5.45	36.14	15.66
	1971	4.85	-	-
Purulia	1991	5.98	31.79	19.11
	1981	5.45	35.79	14.08
	1971	4.64	-	-
Maldah	1991	47.49	36.13	24.44
	1981	45.27	32.27	21.23
	1971	43.13	-	-
Hoogly	1991	14.52	29.15	20.96
	1981	13.76	32.17	22.47
	1971	12.89	-	-
Murshidabad	1991	61.40	34.16	19.60
	1981	58.67	30.67	18.80
	1971	56.34	-	-

Source: Census of India 1991.

* The district has been divided after 1981 census.

age of 25.73 per cent is reached in the districts of Darjeeling, Calcutta and Howrah. Other remaining districts have less than average urban population (see Table 3.8 and Table 3.9).

Table 3.12

Growth of Muslim Population in West Bengal During 1971-81 (less than 30 per cent increase of Muslim population with percentage increase among the Hindus)

District	*Census Year*	*Percentage to Total Muslim Population*	*Percentage Increase*	
			Muslims	*Hindus*
West Dinajpur	1991	36.75	33.55	28.50
	1981	35.79	28.95	29.71
	1971	35.89	-	-
Nadia	1991	24.92	34.49	28.47
	1981	23.87	28.13	26.76
	1971	23.68	-	-
Barddhaman	1991	19.55	38.99	22.42
	1981	17.60	26.59	22.32
	1971	17.17	-	-
Birbhum	1991	33.06	30.15	18.38
	1981	30.98	25.24	14.75
	1971	29.19	-	-
Jalpaiguri	1991	10.04	45.13	22.55
	1981	8.75	23.36	27.57
	1971	8.97	-	-
Kooch Bihar	1991	23.34	37.63	18.56
	1981	20.78	22.52	26.00
	1971	21.25	-	-
Calcutta	1991	17.72	53.75	31.03
	1981	15.34	13.43	3.40
	1971	14.20	-	-

Source: Census of India 1991.

Muslims have increased fast in number particularly in the districts of Darjeeling, Medinipur and Calcutta during 1981-91 census. The growth of Muslim population in Barddhaman is as high as 38.99 per cent. Murshidabad, where Muslims constitute the majority in the population has recorded a growth of 34.16 per cent only, which was below the state average for Muslims, but above the growth rate of the total population.

During 1981-91 Muslims have increased highly in numbers particularly in the districts of Darjeeling (58.55%), Medinipur (53.17%), Murshidabad (34.16%). It is to be noted here that south-west districts, i.e., Medinipur, Bankura and Puruliya Muslim population has increased on a faster rate. On the other hand, it is also to be mentioned that the rate of increase is note-worthy where the Muslims are few in number. We can cite the case of Darjeeling district. Then we can also observe that there is an overall increase in Muslim population in all the districts of West Bengal. Only in the district of Hoogly there is an increase of Muslim population with a low rate---29.15 per cent (see Table 3.11).

Keeping such perspectives in mind, we are to examine the position of the divorced and separated Muslim women in West Bengal. It involves a study of attitudes, practices and the capacity of Muslim women to adopt themselves to the changing social pattern in West Bengal.

4

Status of Women in Islam

Islam originated in Arabia, more particularly in Mecca. It literally means 'peace'. Islam is already 1,400 years old and in India it is at least 1,000 years old. There were trade relations between India and West Asia as early as the semi-historical period of the Babylonian ascendency. Various types of people like Egyptian, Iranian and Arab merchants were constant visitors to the western coast of India. The earliest of such merchants were Shariff, son of Malik, Malik son of Habib and Malik son of Dinar who first landed at Cannanore and succeeded in converting a Hindu chief. But we are to keep in mind that the arrival of the merchants and conversion of a local *raja* was rather accidental.

Through the centuries and years Islam has been able to draw into its unified fold different ethnic and cultural types, all assimilating into a homogenous religious group not merely by force, but by the attraction of a single religious dogma, a simple social pattern and a new attitude to human life which was accepted by a great many men of different ethnic origins and cultural background. According to Shushtery[1], the following are the important causes for the spread of Islam in India:

— The prevalent caste system was unbearable and full of discrimination between low and high classes. By adopting

Islam, members of the lowest caste became entitled to equal status with those belonging to ruling classes. They could inter-marry and could expect promotion to the highest temporal and spiritual ranks in the community.

- Economic condition of the masses.
- Ignorance of their religion on the part of the masses.
- Persecution of non-Muslims by Muslim nobles, generals and rulers in some cases.
- Encouragement given by offering appointment and offices or remission of punishments.
- Missionary activity on the part of thinkers, or Muslim mystics.

Rights of Muslim Women

The status of women in Islam can be properly understood when we are able to know something about their status during pre-Islamic Arabia. Any understanding of its problem must begin with the social situation before the advent of Islam. Now the question is what the status of women was in pre-Islamic Arabian society. Was it better or worse than in the Islamic period? The general impression is that Muslim women enjoyed no rights whatsoever and were treated no better than a commodity. Asghar Ali Engineer[2] opines:

> Although Mecca was an important commercial centre of international dimensions, the tribal social structure had not been dissolved. It continued to be predominant although it was in the process of disintegration. Again the tribal pattern was patriarchal since the known history of the area. As the legend has it Abraham, the chief patriarch of the Jewish tribes had two sons Ishmael and Issac. The Arabs are said to have descended from Ishmael whereas the Jews from Issac. All of them were patriarchal and their value system was accordingly determined.

But many scholars have claimed that there was matriarchy in and around Medina, although they cannot substantiate their arguments. Rodinson[3] argues:

> Scholars like W. Robertson Smith and G.A. Wilken have held the view that traces can be found among the Arabs of that date of the so-called primitive 'matriarchal' stage of society in which women were supposed to have been the dominant sex, with descent reckoned by the mother's side and property (in so far as there was any) handed down through the female line—as for example, from the maternal uncle to his nephew rather than to his son. The existence of any such stage, although once a fashionable theory, has long been acknowledged to be highly improbable; even the idea that the same forms of family life must have persisted in an unvarying pattern throughout the world is, moreover, discounted—in my opinion quite rightly so—by competent experts of the present day. The matriarchal theory has been modified and reduced to a few more or less certain points. It is recognized that there have been human societies in which succession through the maternal line was dominant and that this has sometimes (but by no means always) been associated with a tendency to concede a slightly greater part to women.

He further asserts:

> Some accounts of pre-Islamic Arabia suggest the existence of matrilinear characteristics, especially in some regions, such as Medina. There may be a connection between these characteristics and the traces in certain places of the existence of polyandry, that is, the marriage of one woman to several men at one time. Montgomery Watt has suggested that these disparate signs could be interpreted as an indication that Arab society, which had formerly been matrilinear, was in the Prophet's time in the course of the changing to the patrilinear system, and was, therefore, in a transitional stage associated with the general development towards individualism. This view seems to me, as it does to J. Henninger, somewhat dubious. There is evidence that the patrilinear system predominated in Arabia from time immemorial, in particular from the so-called Thamudic inscriptions. What does seen to be true is that in certain regions and localities such as Medina, this system co-existed with some types of polyandrous

custom, and with the accepted assignation of a substantial role to women (several sources indicate a remote period in which there were Arab queens); even in some cases with uxorilocal residence and the inheritance of property through the female line.

But here we find some ambiguities among the scholars about the property rights of women in pre-Islamic Arabia. While some scholars hold that women enjoyed property rights before the advent of Islam, this is disputed by others. According to the latter, women at that time did not have any property. Their argument is strengthened by the fact that women among pre-Islamic Arabs were included in the property on their father's death and a son could marry his stepmother (Shushtery, 1933). Pre-Islamic Arabs held that the women were inferior to men, were unable to earn their livelihood and defend themselves and their property. Some of the tribes, therefore, killed their daughters for fear of their starvation and of disgrace to themselves on account of them; some of them denied them any inheritance; some of them treated them as chattels to be inherited by the son or the brother of the deceased. In Some tribes, men married their stepmothers and some of them used them as forfeits while gambling. The hiring of wives for a stipulated period was also common among the pre-Islamic Arabs. During this period, Arab women and children could not inherit, because the idea prevailed that inheritance was for those who could fight and defend the family. According to Maulana Muhammad Ali[4]:

> Among the pre-Islamic Arabs, when a man died, his elder son or other relations had a right to possess his widow or widows, marrying them themselves if they pleased, without setting a dowry on them, or marrying them to others, or prohibiting them from marriage altogether.

Some scholars further argue that, as for inheritance, a woman in pre-Islamic Arabia was treated like a commodity. She had no right to inherit from either her husband or father's property or from any other relative. Instead, she herself, in pre-

Islamic Arabia, was an object of inheritance. Engineer[5] opines:

> In the pre-Islamic period, it was generally thought and accepted that inheritance was not meant for women and small children and that it was for those who wield weapons and capture booty, i.e., for the men only.

On the other hand, some scholars have argued that in pre-Islamic Arabia women were generally rich and wealthy, possessed herds and flocks as well as real estate property and carried on flourishing business and trade; and their husbands tended their flocks and worked as their managers. Khadija, the wife of the Prophet, was a rich woman of Mecca who carried on good business. Mawiya, the daughter of Abzar, was a rich princess of Yemen. Among the pre-Islamic Arabs, however, the woman was known as the *Rabbatul-Bayt* or the owner of the house and the husband served as its guard. Burton[6] rightly remarks:

> For the Arab, the tribe to which he was so passionately devoted meant the women of the tribe, his mother, his sister, his wives. His function as a warrior was, by him, chiefly regarded as the defence of the women.

Smith[7] also argued that the position of women in pre-Islamic Arabia was not as inferior as depicted by some scholars. According to him:

> The Arabs jealously watched over their women as their most valuable trust, defended them with their lives and eagerly redeemed them, when they were taken captive.

Among the ancient Arabs the position of the woman was so high that a distinguished French author[8] remarks:

> There is indeed nowhere to be found in the whole range of human records, a nobler type of dignified yet unfettered, free yet self-respecting womanhood than the woman of ancient Arabia, upto the time of decline and fall of Saracenic civilisation. The Spartan mother did not equal her in heroism.

So we may argue that women were not so totally deprived of inheritance in the pre-Islamic period as propounded by some Muslim historians. But there is nothing to deny that men had a greater say and share in this regard and there was no fixed share for women. In this regard, Islam has improved the status of women by giving her property inheritance. Now women came to inherit property along with their male relatives and possess property in their own right. In this connection, Kapadia[9] observes:

> The greatest contribution of Islam to the cause of women was to invest them with property rights.

The rule of the *Quran* guaranteed everyone his share, which was worked out in a somewhat complicated fashion. Women were given the right of inheriting property from their fathers and husbands. It was the custom in Mecca, although not in Medina. That is why, when the right of inheritance by women was first introduced in Medina the people objected vehemently because women did not contribute to the wealth of the tribe or go to battle. The revelation (*Quran*: 4:7,12,176) in its regard came after the death of Aus-bin Thabit whose wife and the three younger daughters were refused any share of Aus' property. Inheritance, technically called *Ilmul-faraez*, is based upon the following text of the *Quran.*[10]

> *Surah 4, 7*
> Men have a share in what the parents and relatives leave behind at death; and women have a share in what the parents and relatives leave behind. Be it large or small a legal share is fixed.

> *Surah 4, 8*
> And when the relatives and orphans and the needy collect at the time of division (of property) provide for them too, and talk kindly to them.

Surah 4, 9
Let people fear the day when they leave small children behind them unprovided and how concerned they would be for them. So fear *Allah* and say the right things to them.

Surah 4, 10
Those who devour the possessions of the orphans unjustly devour only fire, and surely burn in Hell.

Surah 4, 11
As for the children, *Allah* decrees that the share of the male is equivalent to that of two females. If they consist of women only, and of them more than two, they will get two-thirds of the inheritance; but in case there is one, she will inherit one half. The parents will each inherit a sixth of the estate if it happens the deceased has left a child; but if he has left no children; and his parents are his heirs, then the mother will inherit one-third; but if he has left brothers, the mother will inherit one-sixth after payment of legacies and debts. Of parents and children you do not know who are more useful to you. These are the decrees of *Allah* who knows all and is wise.

Surah 4, 12
Your share in the property the wives leave behind is half if they die without an issue, but in case they have left children, then your share is one fourth after the payment of legacies and debts; and your wife shall inherit one-fourth of what you leave at death if you die childless, if not, she will get one-eighth of what you leave behind after payment of legacies and debts. If a man or a woman should die without leaving either children or parents behind but have brother and sister, they shall each inherit one-sixth. In the case there are more, they will share one-third of the estate after payment of legacies and debts without prejudice to others. This is the decree of *Allah* who knows all and is kind.

Surah 4, 176
They ask you for judgement about *Kalalah* (a man who dies childless). Say: "*Allah* has given a decision in the matter of

inheritance." If a man dies and leaves no child behind, but has a sister, she will get a half of what he owned, as he would have done the whole of what she possessed if she had died a childless person. In case he has two sisters then they will get two-thirds of the heritage. But if he has both brothers and sisters the male will inherit a share equal to that of two females. *Allah* makes this manifest to you lest you wander astray, for *Allah* has knowledge of everything.

Islam introduced shares of property for the wife, daughter, sister and grandmother, though admittedly, their share is only half that of the men. A share is even allowed to a son's daughter in the absence of any son of the deceased and the presence of one daughter. The wife, daughter and mother inherit together with the wife being given one-eighth share along with the descendants. If there are no children, or grandchildren, the wife gets one-fourth share. The daughters inherit along with the sons in the ratio of 12 after the prescribed shares of those entitled are settled. A single daughter in the absence of a male issue inherits half the property and two or more daughters receives two-thirds of the property. The mother gets one-sixth along with the descendants and wife (or husband). The mother, along with the father, in the absence of descendants inherits in the proportion of one or two. The grandmother is excluded by the mother and father. In Islam, the descendants as a general rule exclude the ascendants and the ascendants' collaterals. In the *shafi* and *maliki*, the property is shared between grandparents and brothers and sisters, whereas in *Hanafi* school, preference is given to grandparents over collaterals. The shares prescribed by the *Quran* are to be allotted first and then the remaining part of the property passes on to the nearest male agnates.

In Islam, we find a fundamental change in favour of women in that their consent to marriage was made mandatory. Thus no Muslim marriage can be solemnised on the basis of a consent given by the girl's parents or guardians alone. In many cases, she can also contract her marriage, of course through agency of her father or some other paternal relative in the absence of her father. In this regard Shushtery[11] observes:

> Her consent in any case is necessary, though parents are allowed to find a suitable match and even in some cases to force her to give her consent which, however, is not legal.

The pre-Islamic status of women has also been elaborated by Hobhouse. He argues that Islam also gives the Muslim woman the freedom to seek divorce on her own initiative, though it is easier for the male to obtain it. However, for protection from whimsical divorce, the Muslim women have been provided security in the form of *mahr* (the dower) or *sadaq* which she can claim from her husband if she was divorced without any good cause. Even the much maligned phenomenon of 'four wives' is hedged with the qualification that all the wives should be treated equally. The constraints, the apologists of the system point out, have virtually prohibited polygamy. Finally, one other little known privilege is the right to hold public position; indeed, a Muslim women can even act as a judge except where retaliation is involved.

The Prophet very often recommended and pleaded for kind treatment of wives by their husbands, as well as, women in general. This is to be found in the following traditions:

> He said to his followers that 'the best of you is he who is the best to his wife' (Mishkat, Treatment of Women).

> He asked the Muslims to treat their wives well, for they have taken them as a trust from *Allah* (Muslim, Hajj).

> He said that the belief of a Muslim is complete to the extent that he cultivates good habits; and exhibits toleration to his wife (Tirmidhi).

> That the woman is the ruler in the house of her husband (Bukh, Nikah).

> That if you have four *dinars*, spend one of them in holy war waged in self-defence, contribute the second towards setting a slave free, give the third to an orphan and the fourth to your wife, the last will earn you the greatest reward in the eye of *Allah*; that the whole world is useful and the best of it is a good wife (Mishkat, Treatment of Women).

In his oration at the last pilgrimage of Mecca, too, he warned his followers concerning their treatment of their wives and said: "Verily your wives have a right on you, just as you have a right on them."

Relative Status of Muslim Men and Women

Formally, in Islam, men and women stand on equal footing. Woman, like man, is an individual, who can pray to the Almighty, and can hope for redemption. Islam does not consider woman as the root cause of man's downfall. It has given many rights and privileges to the woman. Though Islam has prescribed a much high status to woman than what was commonly prevalent in pre-Islamic Arabian society, yet the standards have hardly kept pace with the times. Therefore, the Muslim *Sharia*, as it has developed over the centuries, places Muslim women in a disadvantageous or in an inferior position to men in many respects. Since, in other matters, e.g., marriage, divorce, social status etc. women's position remained subordinate, their right to hold or inherit property was more nullified in practice than upheld. There have been communities in all parts of the Islamic world, in the past and even now, where the women's rights to property are honoured in breach rather than application.[12]

Asghar Ali Engineer[13] observes:

> It would be erroneous to think that there was all glory for women in Arabia at that time. What has been stated above applies more to influential women or to those women who enjoyed higher social status in the society. The condition of women, in general, was not as happy. Moreover, the women in Bedouin

tribes in desert faced even greater hardships. In the trying conditions of the Arabian desert, women were considered as a burden rather than a supporting hand as in an agricultural society. It was an account of these trying conditions that the female child was considered a burden and, in many cases, even buried alive.

Now the question is that why the condition of Muslim women has been deteriorating with the passage of time. The problem lies with the doctrine of *Ijtihad*, or the principle of movement in religion. In his lectures on 'The Reconstruction of Religious Thought in Islam', Iqbal[14] has pointed out:

> The ultimate spiritual basis of all life, as conceived by Islam, is eternal and reveals itself in variety and change. It must possess eternal principles to regulate its collective life, for the eternal gives us a foothold in the world of perpetual change. But eternal principles, when they are understood to exclude all possibilities of change which, according to the *Quran*, is one of the greatest 'signs' of God, tends to immobilize what is essentially mobile in nature. The failure of Europe in the political and social scene illustrates the former principles, the immobility of Islam during the last 500 years illustrates the latter.

Then, he also argued that:

> The claim of the present generation of Muslim liberals to reinterpret the foundation of legal principles, in the light of their own experience and the altered conditions of modern life is, in my opinion, perfectly justified. The teaching of the *Quran*, that life is a process of progressive creation necessitates that each generation, guided, but unhampered by the work of its predecessors, should be permitted to solve its problems.

And, he goes on to add:

> The closing of the door of *Ijtihad* is pure fiction, suggested partly by the crystallization of legal thought in Islam and partly by the intellectual laziness which, specially in periods of spiritual decay, turns great thinkers into idols.

There is nothing to deny that some provisions and rights have been provided in the *Quran* and *Hadith* for the proper position of Muslim women in society. But it would always be remembered that legal superiority enjoyed by women in a society is not necessarily a true or full index of their social status.[15] Mere 'rights' do not always mean possession. The situation can be illustrated by the following examples:

The Issue of Witness

The question of witness in Islam has been hotly debated among the theologists. Regarding evidence of women in matters of written financial contracts the *Quran*[16] says:

> O believers, when you negotiate a debt for a fixed term, draw up an agreement in writing, though better it would be to have a scribe write it faithfully down; and no scribe should refuse to write as *Allah* has taught him, and write what the borrower dictates, and have fear of *Allah*, his Lord, and not leave out a thing. If the borrower is deficient of mind or infirm, or unable to explain, let the guardian explain judiciously; and have two of your men act as witnesses; but if two men are not available, then a man and two women you approve, so that in case one of them is confused the other may remind her. When the witnesses are summoned they should not refuse (to come).

It means, in regard to witnesses, the *Quran* says that if a second man is not available, two women should be called, so that if one errs, the other will remember or remind her. As far as crimes are concerned, evidence of women is not admissible for it involves 'a degree of doubt'. A woman's evidence is even regarded as a substitute for evidence and if it is to be accepted, it is only where the evidence of men cannot be obtained. In matters relating to property, family and civil law affairs, the law lays down that there should be either two male witnesses or one male and two female witnesses. The evidence of women alone is not admissible on account of their "defect of understanding, their want of memory and incapacity of governing." It suggests that women are unequal in terms of there capabilities and are, therefore, inferior to men. This was used for curtailing the women's right to a minimum in matters of offering evidences in criminal/civil cases.

But this argument has been critically examined, or rather, has been clarified differently from different viewpoints. The stipulation that two women may be substituted for one male witness does not indicate any reflection on woman's moral or intellectual capabilities. The main thing is that the women are unfamiliar with business. Here we are to remember that the clause is a recommendatory and not an obligatory one. In this regard, Engineer[17] opines:

> Another important thing to note about the verse is that though two female witnesses in place of one male witness have been recommended, only one would bear witness, the other's function being nothing more than reminding her in case she falters (on account of her inexperience in financial matters). The words of the *Quran* are *'an tadilla ihdahuma fatudhakkira ihdahumal ukhra*, (if one of them should make a mistake, the other could remind her). In those days there was always some possibility of female witnesses making mistakes in financial matters due to their inexperience and not due to any inferior intellectual ability. This verse should be categorised as a contextual and not a normative one. The *Quran* is certainly not laying down any norm that in matters of witnessing, two would be treated as being equal to one man. Had it been so intended the *Quran*, wherever the question of witnessing arises, would have treated the women in this way. However, this is not so. There are seven other verses about recording evidence in the *Quran*, but none of them lays down the requirement of two female witnesses in place of one man.

Engineer further goes on to say:

> ...in matters of bearing witness women are not second to men as

commonly assumed by the male Muslim jurists relying solely on verse 2:282, while totally ignoring the overwhelming evidence of other *Quranic* verses which make no such discrimination.

Now it is appropriate to quote other verses on the question of witness from the *Quran*. Some scholars argue that Islam does not make any discrimination against women on the question of witness is clearly evident from the following verses. According to them, in all these verses, sex of witness is not specified:

Surah 4, 15
If any of your women is guilty of an immoral act, bring four of your men to give evidence; if they testify against them, retain them in the houses until death, or until *Allah* provide some other way for them.

Surah 4, 35
If you fear a breach between them, appoint one arbiter from the people of the man and one from the people of the woman. If they wish to have a settlement the *Allah* will reconcile them, for *Allah* is all-knowing and cognisant.

Surah 24, 6
Those who accuse their wives and do not have any witnesses except themselves, should swear four times in the name of *Allah*, the testimony of such a person being that he is speaking the truth.

Surah 24, 7
And (Swear) a fifth time that if he lies the curse of *Allah* be on him.

Surah 24, 8
The Woman's punishment can be averted if she swears four times by *Allah* as testimony that her husband is a liar.

Surah 24, 9
Her fifth oath being that the curse of *Allah* be on her if her husband should be speaking the truth.

> *Surah 65, 2*
> When they have reached their appointed time, then either keep them lawfully or let them go honourably; but have two witnesses from among you, and give truthful evidence for (being acceptable to) *Allah*. This is to warn him who believes in *Allah* and the Last Day. *Allah* will furnish a way out for him who fears Him.

These are the relevant verses of the *Quran* on witness. But, in spite of all these verses, the Muslim jurists have deducted a general rule, namely, that one male witness is equal to two women witnesses and argued that man is superior to woman.

Regarding religious duties, both men and women have equal role. But a woman can never be a priest, nor can she lead the prayer. She has no place in the formal organisation of religion and legal affairs of the community,[19] even forever forbidden from attending mosques for public prayers.[20]

Marriage

In Islam, marriage is nothing but a contract. Islamic law permits a man to take as many as four wives at any given time, subject only to the proviso that he must treat all of them equally and justly. Women's legal rights in respect of marriage and divorce are not only inferior to those of men, but are completely out of harmony with the demands of modern time. Religion makes the husband, the family head and expects the wife to obey and serve him.

The *Quran*[21] says:

> And if you have reason to fear that you might not act equitably towards orphans, then marry from among (other) women such as are lawful to you—two, or three, or four; but if you have reason to fear that you might not be able to treat them with equal fairness, then (only) one—or (from among) those whom you rightfully possess. This will make it more likely that you will not deviate from the right course.

Thus, a sociologist says:

> A Muslim man can have up to four wives, with no legal protection to the woman against the exercise of this privilege. The law does not admit polygamy as a cause for seeking divorce by a Muslim woman. Of course, the corresponding right of a woman to have more than one husband in any circumstances is inconceivable, much less is granted under law... A man can divorce at will just by utterings the words 'I divorce you' three times, anywhere, at anytime without any witness. He is also not required by law to give any maintenance to the wife beyond the period of *Iddat*, which is three months and a few days after divorce. If a man divorces his wife, he is obliged to pay *mahr*, a sum of money agreed upon at the time of marriage. This provision is also taken as a security for Muslim women against easy divorce. But as long as the right to have four wives continues to be enjoyed by a man, he need not divorce his wife if he does not wish to pay *mahr* he can simply discard her, or ill; treat her, while taking another wife ... so as to every stage. Muslim law is fettered with inequalities, with the women in every case being less equal.[22]

Many scholars on Islam argue that one of the characteristic features of Islamic law is the unfettered right it gives to the husband to terminate his marriage for any reason or for no reason at all. The law of divorce that was evolved by the Muslim jurists has become the principal sources of suffering for Muslim women. It creates most pitiable conditions for the divorcees and the children. Anderson[23] rightly observes:

> It is true that there are parts of the Muslim world where divorce is commendably rare; but elsewhere it is appallingly common. The Muslim wife indeed has always lived, under the ever present shadow of divorce, a shadow mitigated only in comparatively rare cases by certain pre-cautionary devices ... the unjustified repudiation of a wife is regarded by the jurists, as a sin, but it is nonetheless held to be legally effective.

Bhatty further observes that it would always be remembered that legal superiority enjoyed by women in a society is not necessarily a true or full index of their social status.

Divorce

Now, some understanding is needed of the views expressed in the *Quran* and *Hadith* about divorce. The Muslim law of divorce is founded upon expressed injunctions contained in the *Quran*, as well as in the traditions. Islam permits dissolution or rather break of relations between husband and wife. The Arabic word, *talaq* is usually rendered as 'repudiation', it comes from a root *tollaqa*, which means to release (an animal) from a tether; hence, to repudiate the wife or free her from the bondage of marriage.

The teaching of the *Quran* on the subject is as follows:

The Cow

Surah 2, 226
Those who swear to keep away from their wives (with intent of divorcing them) have four months to grace; then if they reconcile (during this period), surely *Allah* is forgiving and kind.

Surah 2, 227
And they are bent on divorce, *Allah* heeds all and knows everything.

Surah 2, 228
Women, who are divorced, have to wait for three monthly periods, and if they believe in *Allah* and the Last Day they must not hide unlawfully what *Allah* has formed within their wombs. Their husbands would do well to take them back in that case, if they wished to be reconciled. Women also have recognized rights as men have though men have an advantage over them. But *Allah* is almighty and all-wise.

Surah 2, 229
Divorce is (revocable) two times (after pronouncement), after

which (there are two ways open for husbands), either (to) keep (the wives) honourably, or part with them in a decent way. You are not allowed to take away the least of what you have given your wives, unless both of you fear that you would not be able to keep within the limits set by *Allah*. If you fear you can not maintain the bounds fixed by *Allah*, there will be no blame on either if the woman redeems herself. Do not exceed the limits of *Allah*, for those who exceed the bounds set by *Allah* are transgressors.

Surah 2, 230

If a man divorces her again (a third time), she becomes unlawful for him (and he can not marry her) until she has married another man. Then if he divorces her there is no harm if the two unite again if they think they will keep within the bounds set by *Allah* and made clear for those who understand.

Surah 2, 231

When you have divorced your wives, and they have reached the end of the period of waiting, then keep them honourably (by revoking the divorce), or let them go with honour, and do not detain them with the intent of harassing lest you should transgress. He who does so will wrong himself. Do not mock the decrees of *Allah*, and remember the favours *Allah* has bestowed on you of the consequences of doing wrong. Have fear of *Allah* and remember, *Allah* is cognisant of everything.

Surah 2, 232

When you have divorced your wives and they have completed the fixed term (of waiting), do not stop them from marrying other men if it is agreed between them honourably. This warning is for those among you who believe in *Allah* and the Last Day.

This is both proper and right for you, for *Allah* knows and you do not know.

Surah 2, 236

There is no sin in divorcing your wives before the consummation of marriage or setting the dowry; but then provide adequately for them, the affluent according to their means, the poor in accordance with theirs as is befitting. This is surely the duty of those who do good.

Surah 2, 237
And if you divorce them before the consummation of marriage, but after settling the dowry, then half-settled dowry must be paid, unless the woman forgoes it, or the person who holds the bond of marriage pays the full amount. And if the man pays the whole, it is nearer to piety. But do not forget to be good to each other, and remember that *Allah* sees all that you do.

Surah 2, 241
Making a fair provision for women who are divorced is the duty of those who are *Allah*-fearing and pious.

Surah 2, 242
So does *Allah* pronounce His decrees that you may understand.

In the Shah Bano Case, the main problem arises with the interpretation of the two *aiyats* (verses), 241 and 242 of *Surah* 2 of the *Quran*, which argue that there is an obligation on Muslim husbands to provide for their divorced wives. the Arabic version of those *aiyats* and their English translations are as follows:[24]

Arabic Version	*English Version*
aiyat 241	
Wa lil motallaqatay	For divorced women
mataun	Maintenance (should be provided)
bil maaroofay	On a reasonable scale
haqqan	This is a duty
alal muttaqeena	On the righteous.
aiyat 242	
Kazaleka yubaiyyanullaho	Thus doth *Allah*
lakum ayatehee la allakum	Make clear His signs.
taqeloon	To you; in order that you may understand.

To some, the main problems arise with the word, *Mata,* in *aiyat* 241 which means 'provision' and not 'maintenance'. For having some clear idea of these two *aiyats* we can quote some translations done by some learned scholars on the subject.

The translation of *aiyats* 240 to 242 in the meaning of the *Quran*[25] reads thus:

> Those of you, who shall die and leave wives behind them, should make a will to the effect that they should be provided with a year's maintenance and should not be turned out of their homes. But if they leave their homes of their own accord, you shall not be answerable for whatever they choose for themselves in a fair way; *Allah* is All powerful, All-wise. (likewise, the divorced women should also be given something in accordance with the known fair standard. This is an obligation upon the *Allah*-fearing people.)
>
> *Surah 2, 242*
> Thus *Allah* makes clear His commandments for you; it is expected that you will use your common sense.

Allama Abdullah Yusuf Ali's translation[26] runs as follows:

> *Surah 2, 241*
> For divorced women maintenance (would be provided) on a reasonable (scale). This is a duty on the righteous.

Marmaduke Pickthall[27] reads it as:

> *Surah 2, 241*
> For divorced women a provision in kindness: A duty for those who ward off (evil).

Then again, we find some provisions on *talaq* in the chapter 4 under the heading, 'The Women':

> *The Women*
> *Surah 4, 35*
> If you fear a breach between them appoint one arbiter from the

people of the man and one from the people of the woman. If they wish to have a settlement then *Allah* will reconcile them, for *Allah* is all-knowing and cognisant.

Surah 4, 128
If a woman fears ill-treatment from her husband or his tiring of her, there is no harm if they make a peaceful settlement, and peace is an excellent thing. Yet avarice is part of man's nature. If you do good and fear *Allah*, *Allah* is cognisant of all that you do.

Surah 4, 130
If both (decide to) separate, *Allah* in his largesse will provide for them; for *Allah* is infinite and all-wise.

Then again, in the chapter 'The Allied Troops' we find:

Surah 33, 49
O you who believe, when you marry believing women then divorce them before having (sexual) contact with them, you have no right to demand observance of the 'Waiting Period' of them. But provide suitably for them, and let them go with honour.

In chapter 65 of the *Quran* there are also some provisions on *talaq*:

Divorce
Surah 65, 1
O prophet when you divorce women, divorce them at their appointed period, and calculate that period, and fear *Allah*, your lord. Do not expel them from their houses, nor should they go away themselves, unless they are openly guilty of adultery. These are the limits set by *Allah*. And any one who exceeds the limits set by *Allah* sins against his own self.

Surah 65, 2
When they have reached their appointed time, then either keep them lawfully or let them go honorably; but have two witnesses from among you, and give truthful evidence for (being acceptable to) *Allah*. This is to warn him who believes in *Allah* and the Last

Day. *Allah* will furnish a way out for him who fears Him.

Surah 65, 4

As for your women who have lost hope of menstruation, and in case you have a doubt, the prescribed period (of waiting) for them is three months, as also for those who have not menstruated yet. As for those who are pregnant, their prescribed period is until the delivery of the child. *Allah* will make things easy for him who is mindful of *Allah*.

Surah 65,6

House the (divorced) women where you live, according to your means; but do not harass them so as to reduce them to straitened circumstances. If they are pregnant, then spend on them until they give birth to the child. And if they suckle the child for you, then make the due payment to them, and consult each other appropriately. But if you find this difficult, let some other woman suckle (the child) for her.

Surah 65,7

Let the man of means spend according to his means, and he whose means are limited, should spend of what *Allah* has given him. *Allah* does not burden a soul beyond what He has given him. *Allah* will bring ease after hardship.

From the above discussion we can broadly mention different modes of divorce. The contract of marriage in Islam may be dissolved in any one of the following ways: (1) by the husband at his will, without the intervention of a court; (2) by mutual consent of the husband and wife, without the intervention of the court; and (3) by a judicial decree at the suit of the husband or wife. The wife cannot divorce herself from her husband without his consent, except under a contract whether made before or after marriage, but she may, in some cases, obtain a divorce by judicial decree.

We are to remember that when the divorce proceeds from the husband, it is called *talaq*; when it is effected by mutual consent, it is called *khula* or *mubara'at* according to the terms of the contract between the parties.

Any Muslim of sound mind, who has attained puberty, may divorce his wife whenever he desires without assigning any cause.

A *talaq* may be effected (i) orally (by spoken words), or (ii) by a written document called a *talaqnama*.

In oral *talaq*, no particular form of words is prescribed for effecting a *talaq*. Some Mohammedan jurists argue that if the words are expressed (*saheeh*) or well understood as implying divorce no proof of intention is required. If the words are ambiguous (*kinayat*) the intention must be proved. This argument has been given in the following cases: Ma Mi vs. Kallandar Ammal, supra; Asha Bibi vs. Kadir (1909) 33 Mad. 22, 3 I.C. 730; Wahid Khan vs. Zainab Bibi (1914) 36 All. 458, 25 I.C. 387; Ibrahim vs. Syed Bibi (1888) 12. Mad. 63. On the other hand, it is not necessary that the *talaq* should be pronounced in the presence of the wife or even addressed to her. What is required most is to name the wife. In a Calcutta case (Furzund Hussein vs. Janu Bibee (1878) 4 Cal. 588) the husband merely pronounced the word "*talaq*" before a family council and this was held to be invalid as the wife was not named. If the *talaq* pronounced in the absence of the wife takes effect though not communicated to her, but for purposes of dower it is necessary that it should come to her knowledge (Fulchand vs. Nazib Ali, supra); and her alimony may continue till she is informed of the divorce (Ma Mi vs. Kallandar Ammal, supra; Abdul Khader vs. Azeaza Bee (1944) I M.L.J. 17, 214 I.C 38, (1944). A.M. 227.)

Talaq in writing: A *talaqnama* may only be the record of the fact of an oral *talaq*; or it may be the deed by which the divorce is effected. The deed may be executed in the presence of the *Qazi* (Sarabai vs. Rabiabai(1905) 30 Bom. 537) or of the wife's father (Waj Bibee vs. Azmut Ali (1868) 8 W.R. 23) or of other witnesses (Rajasaheb, In re (1920) 44, Bom. 44, 54 I.C. 573; Ahmad Kasim vs. Khatoon Bibi (1932) 59 Cal. 833. The deed is said to be in the customary form if it is properly superscribed and addressed so as to show the name of the writer and the person addresse. If it is not so superscribed and addressed it is said to be in unusual form. If the deed is in customary form and manifest, the intention to divorce is presumed. Otherwise, the intention to divorce must be proved. It is to be noted here that communication within a reasonable time is not necessary and the *talaqnama* operates from the date of execution. If an acknowledgment of divorce is made by the husband, the divorce will be held to take effect at least from the date upon which the acknowledgment is made (Asmat Ullah vs. Khatun-un-nisa [1939) All. 763 (1939) A.L.J. 804, 184 I.C. 517, (1939) A.A. 592]

Ram Malik[28] and Mulla's[29] Principles of Mahomedan Law discussed divorce under three broad headings: *ahasan talaq*, *hasan talaq* and *talaq-al-bida*.

To divorce his wife, according to the most acceptable form, *ahasan talaq*, the husband utters a single word, *talaq* and abstains from marital intercourse with her for a period of three months during which reconciliation is possible and the divorce revocable. If the husband explicitly revokes it by resuming cohabitation, the effect of the *talaq* is nullified and the marriage continues. If the husband does not revoke the *talaq* during the said period, the divorce becomes final at the end of the three months.

M. Hidayatullah opines that when the marriage has not been consummated, a *talaq* in the *ahsan* form may be pronounced even if the wife is in her menstruation.

Where the wife has passed the age for periods of menstruation the requirement of a declaration during a *tuhr* (period between menstruation) is inapplicable; further more, this requirement only applies to an oral divorce and not a divorce in writing.

The less approved form of divorce (*hasan talaq*) involves a procedure by which the husband pronounces a *talaq* once a month for three consecutive months. According to some Mohammedan jurists, this consists of three pronouncements made during successive *tuhrs*, no intercourse taking place during any of the three *tuhrs*. The first pronouncement should be made during a *tuhr*, the second during the next *tuhr*, and the third during the succeeding *tuhr*.

The most reprehensible form of divorce and, by far, the most common (*talaq-ul-bidaat* or *talaq-i-badai*) is when the husband simply makes three pronouncements immediately during a single *tuhr* either in one sentence, e.g., "I divorce thee thrice", or in separate sentence, e.g., "I divorce thee, I divorce thee, I divorce thee" [Amir-ud-din vs. Khatun Bibi (1917) 39 All. 39 I.C. 513].

On the other hand, a single pronouncement made during a *tuhr* clearly indicates an intention irrevocably to dissolve the marriage e.g., "I divorce thee irrevocably". [Sarabhai vs. Rabiabai(1905) 30 Bom. 537].

The *Hanafis* recognise two kinds of *talaq*, namely, (a) *talaq-us-sunnat*, that is, *talaq* according to the rules laid down in the *sunnat*, i.e., traditions of the Prophet; and (b) *talaq-ul-bidaat*, i.e., new or irregular *talaq*. Some jurists call it *talaq al-bid'ah*, i.e., innovative form of divorce. *Talaq-ul-bidaat* was first introduced by the *Omeyyade* monarchs in the second century of the Mohammedan era. Some scholars argued that *talaq-ul-bidaat* is good in law, though bad in theology, and it is the most common and prevalent mode of divorce among the *Sunni* Muslims in our country. There are the differences among the great Islamic jurists regarding its permissibility. Imam Abu Hanafi and Imam Malik, two great jurists of Islam, argue that the three divorcee in one sitting is *bid'ah*, i.e., an innovation and so this form of divorce is not permissible. Whereas Imam Shafa'i, the fourth great Imam and jurist, thinks that this form of divorce is permissible and is the husband's right.

Talaq-us-sunnat is of two kinds, namely, (a) *ahsan*, that is most proper, and (b) *hasan*, that is, proper. In the case of *talaq ahsan* and *talaq hasan*, the husband has an opportunity of reconsidering his decision, for the *talaq* in both these cases does not become absolute until a certain period had elapsed, and the husband has the option to revoke it before then.

Now, the question is when *talaq* becomes irrevocable. These are as follows:

A *talaq* in the *ahsan* mode becomes irrevocable and complete on the expiration of the period of *iddat*.

A *talaq* in the *hasan* mode becomes irrevocable and complete on the third pronouncement.

A *talaq* in the *badai* mode becomes irrevocable immediately after it is pronounced. There is no need for waiting the *iddat* period in this case. As it becomes irrevocable immediately, it is called *talaq-i-bain*, that is, irrevocable *talaq*.

Islam also retained the women's right to divorce. In Islam a marriage may be dissolved not only by *talaq*, which is the arbitrary act of the husband, but also by agreement between the husband and wife. A dissolution of marriage by agreement may take the form of *khula* or *mubara'at*. This type of divorce is effected by an offer from the side of wife to compensate the husband if he releases her from his marital rights and acceptance by the husband of the offer. Once the offer is accepted by the husband, it operates as a single irrevocable divorce i.e. *talaq-i-bain* and its operation is not postponed until execution of the *khulanama* (deed of the *khula*).

A divorce by *khula* is a divorce with the consent, and at the instance of the wife, in which she gives or agrees to give a consideration to the husband for her release from the marriage tie. In such a case, the terms of the bargain are matters of arrangement between the husband and wife, and the wife may, as the consideration, release her *dyn-mahr* (dower) and other rights, or make any other agreement for the benefit of the husband (Monshee Buzul-ul-Raheem vs. Luteefutoon-Nisa (1861) 8 M.I.A. 379, 395). Failure on the part of the wife to pay the consideration for the divorce does not invalidate the divorce [(1861) 8 M.I.A. 379, 397-398 supra], though the husband may sue the wife for it.

Some jurists agree that if woman seeks divorce she is not entitled to get back the *mahr* money.

So we can argue that the *Quran* is explicit on the conditions of divorce as well as the possibility of reconciliation. Mohammedan interpreters argue that the prescribed time mentioned in the *Quran* is a period of roughly three months which serves the dual purpose of allowing temper to cool and for pregnancy to be established.

Except in the case of adultery, the husband cannot turn the wife out of his house until the period of *iddat* has expired. Punishment of such act is severe, but the establishment of the fact of adultery is not easy. The *Quran* is very specific regarding such act. It observes:

> And those who accuse honourable women, but bring not four witnesses, scourge them (with) eight stripes and never (afterwards) accept their testimony. They, indeed, are evil-doers.[30]

Mohammedan doctors opine that Islam calls for enough thought before the final announcement of *talaq*. It is found that Islam forbids remarriage between a divorced couple until the woman has not only married someone else, but the marriage has been consummated. Thus we find a *Hadith* in Bukhari to this effect. A person divorced his wife thrice; she then married another person who also happened to divorce her. The Holy Prophet was asked whether she could marry her former husband. The Prophet said not until her second husband had had physical intimacy with her as the former husband had.[31] So the scholars argue that it is nothing but a deterrent to thoughtless divorce.

Regarding *talaq* the Prophet had a mixed reaction. The teaching of the Prophet Mohammed on the general subject of divorce is expressed in the traditions as follows:

> The thing which is lawful but disliked by *Allah* is divorce. There are three things which, whether done in jest or in earnest, shall be

considered serious and effectual, namely, marriage, divorce and taking a wife back.
Every divorce is lawful except a mad man's.
Cursed be the second husband who makes the wife (divorced) lawful for her first husband, and cursed be the first husband for whom she is made lawful (*Mishkat, XIIIe.XV*).

The Prophet is reported to have conveyed his indignation to a man who pronounced three *talaqs* in one sitting (*Nasa'i*) and annulled a *talaq* pronounced three times without intervals (Ibn Hanbal). The prophet is reported to have also disapproved of women demanding *talaq* from their husbands without sufficient reasons. A tradition laid down that the three *talaqs* should be pronounced during the three periods of purity (i.e., the non-menses period) and the husband should not have any intercourse during these periods to make the *talaq* binding and irrevocable (Bukhari).[33]

From this general understanding, we may analyse the position and status of divorced and separated Muslim women in West Bengal. The Muslim women have been given some rights and privileges in the *Quran* and *Hadith*. But the question is, how far are these effective in practice? And, therefore, to understand the real position of the divorced and separated Muslim women in West Bengal, we need to know the dialectics between divorced and separated Muslim women in West Bengal and their religious life and, thereby, the relation between them.

Notes

1. A.M.A. Shushtery (1992): *Outlines of Islamic Culture*, Bangalore: Bangalore Printing and Publishing Company, pp. 22-23.
2. Asghar Ali Engineer (ed.) (1987): *Status of Women in Islam*, Delhi: Ajanta Publication, pp. 80-81.

3. Maxime Rodinson (1971): *Mohammed*, England: Penguin Books Limited, pp. 229-230.
4. Maulana Muhammad Ali (1978): *Holy Quran*, English Translation with Arabic Text, Lahore, p. 194.
5. Asghar Ali Engineer (1992): *The Rights of Women in Islam*, New Delhi: Sterling Publishers Private Limited, p. 31.
6. Quoted in Dr. M.Z. Siddiqi: *Sir Abdullah Memorial Lectures on The Social Position of Woman Through the Ages*, Calcutta: Calcutta University, pp. 14-15.
7. Ibid, p. 15.
8. Ibid, p. 13.
9. K.M. Kapadia (1982): *Marriage and Family in India*, Oxford: Oxford University Press, p.198.
10. *The Quran*: Surah 4:7-12, Surah 176.
11. Ibid, pp. 397-398.
12. S.T. Lokhandwala (1987): "The Position of Women Under Islam" in Asghar Ali Engineer (ed.): *Status of Women in Islam*, New Delhi: Ajanta Publication, p. 71.
13. Asghar Ali Engineer: Ibid, p. 82.
14. Quoted by K.G. Saiyidain in S.T. Lokhandwala (ed.) (1971): *India and Contemporary Islam*, Simla: Indian Institute of Advanced Study.
15. Zarina Bhatty (1976): "Status of Muslim Women and Social Change" in B.N. Nanda (ed.): *Indian Women: From Purdah to Modernity*, New Delhi: Vikas Publishing House.
16. *The Quran*: Surah: 2: 282.
17. Asghar Ali Engineer (1992): op.cit., p. 64.
18. Justice Aftab Hussain (1987): *Status of Women in Islam*, Lahore, p. 278.
19. Government of India (1971): *Towards Equality: Report of Committee on the Status of Women in India*, Delhi: Ministry of Education and Social Welfare.
20. Asghar Ali Engineer (1992): op.cit., p. 91.

21. *The Quran*: Surah 4:3.
22. Zarina Bhatty (1976): op. cit., p. 102.
23. J.N.D. Anderson (1959): *Islamic Law in the Modern World*, New York: New York University Press, pp. 51-52.
24. Quoted in Shah Bano Case (1986): *Shariat and The Muslim Women (Protection of Rights on Divorce) Act*, Published by the Judicial Department, Government of West Bengal.
25. Board of Islamic Publication: *The Meaning of the Quran*, Vol. I, Delhi.
26. Allama A. Yusuf Ali (1982): *The Meaning of the Illustrious Quran*, New Delhi: Kitab Bhavan.
27. Marmaduke Pickthall: *The Meaning of the Glorious Quran*, Text and Explanatory Translation, Karachi: Tax Company Limited.
28. Ram Malik (1987): *Nari Samaj O Islami Siksha* (in Bengali), Dhaka: Islamic Foundations, p. 144.
29. M. Hidayatullah (1972): *Mulla's Principles of Mahomedan Law*, Bombay: N.M. Tripathi Private Limited, p. 297.
30. *The Quran*: Surah 24:4.
31. Asghar Ali Engineer (1992): op. cit., pp. 123-124.
32. Quoted in S.T. Lokhandwala(1987): op. cit., p.61.

5

Family, Marriage and Divorce among the Bengali Muslims

"The theory of Islam", observes Levy[1], "...regards the empire of Islam as a theocracy, in which *Allah* as a supreme ruler is also the true law giver. Mohammed the Prophet was the agent through whom believers were made aware explicitly or implicitly, embodied in the *Quran* and his (the Prophet's) *sunna*, of the sum-total of his ordinary doings and saying upon them in turn the *shar* or *shari'a*, by hypothesis, is founded.

And, the Muslims of Islamic countries accept *Shari'a* to be the guiding principle on the question of their religious and social life and seek to abide by it. The word *sunna* or tradition means the trodden path. It denotes some kind of practice and precedent. The word *sunna* was first applied to custom and to the practice of the early schools of Mohammedan law, and finally it means the practice and precedents of the Prophet. The principles which were stated in the *Quran* found their application in the hands of the Prophet. This gave birth to *hadis* (practice - Pl. *ahadis*) of the Prophet. We are to remember here that as a source of law *hadis* is as binding on the believers of Islam as the principles of *Quran*. According to Mulla's Principles of Mohammedan Law,[2] the term *sunna* is sometimes applied to the precedents created by authorities other than the Prophet, but this is a wrong use of the term and is best avoided. The number of *ahadis* is very large. Ahmed ibn-Hanbal in his *Musnad* collected over 80,000 *ahadis*. The authoritative collections in this regard are *Bukhari, Muslim, Ibn Maja, Nasai, Sanin Kubra*, etc.

The *Shari'a* or the law of Islam distinguishes between what is *sahih* (lawful) and what is *batal* (forbidden). Some acts are termed rights of *Allah* and others, rights of men. The former again are classified into complete and partial; likewise the latter.

In this regard, the greatest difference between the *Sunnis* and *Shias* lies in the fact that the *Shias* do not give credence to a *hadis* unless it emanates from the household of the Prophet, particularly from the household of Ali.

It is commonly understood that Muslims in India are strictly following the basic tenets of Islam as embodied in two sources, namely, the *Quran* and *Sunna*. The understanding has been widely accepted by both the sociologists and social anthropologists, and by the common people also. But every religion of the world has its cultural variation. Local practices, rituals, belief system and such other related things have been incorporated in all religions of the world. No religion in the world can ignore the importance of such belief system and practices of the people.

And throughout the ages these belief patterns and practices have become important elements and parts of religions. Here we are to analyse such variations among the Bengali Muslims on the question of social institutions, marriage, divorce, etc.

Like all other Indian communities, the basic unit of the kinship system among the Bengali Muslims is the household which they usually call *ghar*. It refers to a residential and domestic unit comprising the person or persons living together under the same roof and eating food cooked in a common kitchen. Here both the nuclear as well as joint family structures are noticeable. The Bengali Muslims are a patrilineal community and the mode of residence at marriage is patrilocal.

Marriage

As with all other community people, marriage among Bengali Muslims is looked upon as essential and compulsory for both males and females. In Islam, marriage is a civil contract made by mutual consent between man and woman. Among the *Sunni* Muslims, the presence of two male, or one male and two female witnesses and a dower are necessary. Both the bride and bridegroom can stipulate conditions for marriage. A Muslim marriage has fixed and rigid rules which were laid down and practised by the Prophet. It is essential for the validity of a marriage that there should be a proposal made by or on behalf of one of the parties to the marriage, and an acceptance of the proposal by or on behalf of the other, in the presence and hearing of two males or one male and two female witnesses, who must be sane and adult Muslims. The proposal and acceptance must both be expressed at one meeting; a proposal made at one meeting and an acceptance made at another meeting do not constitute a valid marriage. Shushtery[3] opines:

> A woman who has reached the age of puberty is free to choose, to accept or to refuse an offer, although such conduct may be against the declared wishes of her parents or guardians. If a woman was married in her infancy, she may renounce and dissolve the contract on reaching her majority. Her consent in any case is necessary, though parents are allowed to find a suitable match and even in some cases to force her to give her consent, which, however, is not legal. She can make her own terms before the marriage, as to the amount of the dowry to be paid to her, the dissolution of marriage in case her husband leaves the place and goes to some other country or in regard to any other matter. All terms and conditions agreed to mutually would be binding on the husband. Freedom, age and health are the conditions for a marriage.

In spite of the Prophet's preaching of equality, selection of spouses is restricted within one's religious sect and larger kinship group. Muslim parents are said to be 'not free' unless they see their sons and daughters get married. It is also looked upon as a *sunna* and therefore it is regarded as an obligation which must be fulfilled. It is to be noted that when the daughters reach their marriageable age, a suitable match has to be found out for them.

Some scholars argue that marriages between parallel cousins and cross-cousins were preferred due to their weak economic position. There is also a view that to keep family property intact, Muslims prefer marriages between close relatives. Shushtery[4] opines:

> Marriage between cousins, both on the paternal and maternal sides, is permitted in Islam. Among the Arabs and the Iranians, a man had the right to claim the hand of his cousin, because the property, in such a case, would continue to remain in the same family and, if the family is not rich, the purity of blood also be preserved. The Iranians prefer first cousins because of the feeling that where husband and wife are of equal status and possess the same family ties, harmony of life and domestic happiness would result.

In our present study, we have found that regarding mate selection majority of the parents prefer the working capacity or rather good physique of the bridegroom. Out of the total 128 respondents interviewed in our field studies, 29 respondents have no guardians. From a total of 99 parents, 56 respondents gave highest priority to physical capacity of the bridegroom in both the districts. Next in order of preference came property consideration.

In Table 5.1 we find that in both the *gram panchayats*, i.e., Mongolkote *gram panchayat* of Barddhaman district and Panchthupi *gram panchayat* of Murshidabad district, there were five cases where preference was given for blood relation and one each in both districts where preference was given for service in mate selection. And this mate selection was very much restricted within the neighbouring villages because of their poor economic condition.

Table 5.1

Parents' Mode of Preference Regarding the Selection of Daughter's Mate

Preferences	*Murshidabad*		*Barddhaman*		*Total*	
	n	%	*n*	%	*n*	%
Health	24	41.3	32	45.71	56	43.75
Property	11	18.9	10	14.29	21	16.41
Daughter's choice	06	10.34	06	8.57	12	9.37
Relative	04	6.90	01	1.43	05	3.91
Education	01	1.72	02	2.86	03	2.34
Service	01	1.72	01	1.43	02	1.56
N.A.	11	18.97	18	25.71	29	22.65
Total	58	100.00	70	100.00	128	100.00

A number of interesting conclusions can be drawn from Table 5.1. We can see that a large portion of the interviewed persons from both districts placed a great emphasis on the health of the prospective groom. Importance was attached to his property, but surprisingly even educational qualification and white-collar job status of the groom were hardly taken into account. These are no doubt important indicators of the socio-economic conditions prevailing among the Muslims in West Bengal villages.

Formerly, the age of marriage was extremely low among the Bengali Muslims. Many old people speak of themselves and others whom they knew being married at a very early age. Even today the picture has not changed remarkably. If we take note of Table 5.2, we find that in Murshidabad 5.17 per cent respondents and in Barddhaman 8.57 per cent respondents got married at a very early age, i.e., 10 years on average. And 41.38 per cent in Murshidabad and 54.28 per cent in Barddhaman got married in the age group of 10-15 years; 35.16 per cent in both districts got married in the age of group of 15-20 years and the remaining 9.37 per cent got married at the age group of 20 years and above.

Table 5.2

Respondents' Age at the Time of Marriage

Age	*Murshidabad*		*Barddhaman*		*Total*	
	n	%	*n*	%	*n*	%
10 years	03	5.17	06	8.57	09	7.03
10-15 years	24	41.38	38	54.28	62	48.44
15-20 years	21	36.21	24	34.28	45	35.16
20-25 years	09	15.52	01	1.43	10	7.81
25-30 years	01	1.72	01	1.43	02	1.56
Total	58	100.00	70	100.00	128	100.00

One clear fact thus emerges from Table 5.2. It can be easily seen that child marriage or at least marriage before the legally permissible minimum age of the interviewed married women, was widespread in both the districts. In fact, more than 46.55 per cent in Murshidabad and nearly 62.86 per cent girls in Barddhaman were married off before they reached the age of 15 years. The difference between the respective figures in Barddhaman and Murshidabad is also noteworthy and appears to be significant.

Negotiations

An important part of marriage negotiations is making the formal proposal. Traditionally, the woman herself is not allowed to negotiate her marriage. She is given into marriage by her guardian (*wali*), who generally happens to be her father. In the absence of her father, her paternal grandfather and brother and other male relations on the father's side, in the order of inheritance, act as guardian.

Marriage negotiations can be carried out by both the families of the boy and the girl, but the formal proposal depends only on the boy's family. In general, the parents of the girl start negotiations and send a marriage proposal to the boy's parents or elders in the family. This is done through a close relative or friend of the family, or sometimes through the elderly people of the village. The Bengali Muslims hold the idea that the marriage of an individual (girl) should be arranged by her parents, or by her senior relatives in case her parents are not alive. Among the Bengali Muslims, there is no existence of *ghatak* or match-maker as in the case of Hindus. Tables 5.3 and 5.4 below show that this practice is usually being followed even now.

Table 5.3

Parents' Attitude Towards Taking Daughter's Consent at her Marriage

Attitude	*Murshidabad*		*Barddhaman*		*Total*	
	n	%	*n*	%	*n*	%
Taken	26	44.83	38	54.29	64	50.00
Not taken	21	36.20	11	15.71	32	25.00
Did not feel need	00	00.00	03	4.29	03	2.34
N.A.	11	18.97	18	25.71	29	22.66
Total	58	100.00	70	100.00	128	100.00

Table 5.4

Mode of Arrangement of Marriage

Mode of Arrangement	*Murshidabad*		*Barddhaman*		*Total*	
	n	%	*n*	%	*n*	%
By parents	52	89.65	64	91.4	116	90.6
By respondents	06	10.35	06	8.6	12	9.4
Total	58	100.00	70	100.00	128	100.00

We see from Table 5.3 that 50 per cent of the interviewed parents were in favour of taking their daughter's consent. However, it is not consistent with the findings of Table 4.2, where we find that early marriage is widespread in both the districts and hence, it appears strange that parents would have sought their 10-year-old daughter's consent at her marriage. However, our survey reveals that only 26 out of 58 parents (44.83%) in Murshidabad took the consent of the daughter to marriage. The corresponding figure for Barddhaman is much higher, nearly 54.29 per cent (the above data relate to information provided by the divorced/separated women themselves). When the parents were interviewed, the same question evoked different responses. However, the differences can be ignored. It is likely that mandatory consent sought from the bride at the time of marriage was considered equivalent to consultation regarding her marriage. Engineer[5] rightly observes:

> ...the *Jahiliyah* practice of contracting marriage by her *wali* (marriage guardian) on her behalf re-established itself and her approval was reduced to a mere nod or silence. From playing an active role in marriage she came to be relegated to passive position.

Dowry

In Islam, there is no provision for dowry. Rather it is the womenfolk who are supposed to get *mahr* or dower, i.e., bride money agreed upon at the time of marriage. But among the Bengali Muslims, the practice of dowry is widely prevalent whatever be their socio-economic status. The amount of dowry is decided before the date of marriage is fixed which varies from place to place. If we take note of our survey then we find that the parents of 78.13 per cent respondents had to pay dowry in the *gram panchayats* of both the districts. Only 4.3 per cent in Murshidabad had taken it and 9.53 per cent had not given or taken any dowry money. Again, regarding the amount of dowry, it varied from cash to ornaments to land. Out of a total 128 respondents, 54 had to pay cash. Among these 54 respondents, 24 belonged to the district of Barddhaman and 30 respondents were from Murshidabad. One respondent in each district had to give ornaments as dowry, 21 respondents of each district had to pay both cash and ornaments. One respondent in Murshidabad and two respondents in Barddhaman had to give land as dowry. It is thus quite clear that the practice of dowry is prevalent and kicking in the Muslim community of West Bengal. Since the survey was conducted in a rural setting, we find that land (along with cash) is an important mode of payment of dowry.

The Ceremony

The essential element of the wedding ceremony among the Bengali Muslims is the '*nikah*'. Bengali Muslims perform the *nikah* ceremony to solemnise their marriage and the form of the ceremony is the same as one prescribed by Islam. But the wedding is preceded by various kinds of rituals and practices. The women of the village start singing songs in the house of both the bride and bridegroom in the evening which they themselves compose in their own dialect. In such songs, events in the surrounding villages and current political issues play a very important role. Three days before the marriage, the bridegroom's family usually sends '*lagan*' (a box-load of sarees and cosmetics) to the bride's family. And the day before the marriage in both houses, the rituals of '*tel-halood*' and '*aiburo bhat*' are followed. At mid-day, before the day of marriage, women of all ages gather in the house where the wedding is taking place, in the central place in the house where the bride/bridegroom is seated. All women present in the house place their palms on the head of the bride/the bridegroom and the mother pours down coconut oil. Then the women circle the bride/the bridegroom seven times and sing different kinds of marriage songs. The bride/bridegroom is then anointed with *halood* and the women of the houses distribute some dry food among those who come to attend the ceremony.

'*Aiburo bhat*' ceremony is the last ritual of having rice before marriage. Whatever may be its socio-economic position, the family of the bride/groom prepares the best food it can and serves the bride or bridegroom in the evening. The elderly male and female relatives as well as people or neighbours who are present at the ceremony/feed the bride/bridegroom and offer some gifts. The gifts include sarees, ornaments and cash. And as the entire ceremony continues, women in the family and neighbourhood sing songs and enjoy jokes.

The chief function of the marriage, according to Islam, is the ceremony of *nikah*, which means conjunction, and is understood in the sense of contract. In this ceremony, the *maulana* or *qazi* sits in front of the bridegroom surrounded by all the invited friends, relations and parents of the bride and the bridegroom. It is a simple ceremony, for which the assent of the man and woman to marry each other is necessary. Two adult males must be witnesses and the amount of *mahr* payable must be fixed. These two witnesses approach the girl and first seek her consent to marriage. The girl is seated in the middle of the house or in some suitable place, dressed in her best, surrounded by her friends or elderly women of the house. Her father or mother or brother usually tells her to give her consent after the announcement of the proposal by one of the witnesses. As soon as she gives her consent to the wedding, the witnesses leave for the place where the bridegroom is seated. They declare in the *majlis* (gathering) that the daughter has given her consent to the marriage. Similar affirmation is then sought from the boy. Once the consent of both the boy and girl is obtained, the *maulana* or *qazi*, recites a few passages from the *Quran* and tradition in praise of sexual relations, and ends with blessing for both, in which the others present also join.

Mahr or Dower

But as soon as *nikah* has been read, the bridegroom's father is required to fix the *mahr*. *Mahr*, which is also known as *sadaq* is an essential part of Islamic marriage. Without *mahr* a *nikah* cannot be said to have been properly solemnised. A man asks for the hand of a woman from a man, pays *sadaq* (dower money) and marries her. Its origin is pre-Islamic and tribal and it is essentially a bride-price, but Islam elevated it from being merely a bride-price to being a token of love, truthfulness and sincerity. Most of the *Quarashites* and other tribes followed similar customs. In pre-Islamic Arabia, it was given to the family of the woman for offering her hand in marriage. There was a basic difference between *mahr* and *sadaq*. The former was paid to the marriage-guardian (i.e., *wali*) and the latter to the bride herself.[6]

Mahr, or dower, is a sum of money or other property which the wife is entitled to receive from the husband at the time of marriage. It is to be paid or fixed before the solemnization of marriage and it is the exclusive preserve of the bride to determine the amount. The *mahr* amount paid to her is her own. Neither her father nor her husband can claim it. She alone owns it in her own right.[7] The *Quran* repeatedly exhorts men to give *mahr* to the women they intend to marry. It says:

> And give women their dowries as a free gift. But if they of themselves be pleased to give you a portion thereof, consume it with enjoyment and pleasure.[8]

It means, *mahr* should be a free gift and the husband can enjoy it only if the wife permits it, not otherwise.

The amount of money fixed for *mahr* varies from 1¼ *surkh dinar* to any amount---1¼ surkh dinar is the *Sharai mahr* or the *mahr* which is adjusted as the ideal amount fixed by the Prophet. In the present survey the highest amount of *mahr* money was Rs 50,000. The families of the *Maulana* and *Maulvi* and some religious minded people of every society fix a *sharai mahr*. But in all other cases, the amount of *mahr* depends on the girl's family status. The more financially well established and renowned the family is, the more is the amount of *mahr* fixed. Some people consider it as security for woman and fix large sum of money as *mahr*. "Dower is often high among Mohammedans, to prevent the husband from divorcing his wife, in which case he would have to pay the amount stipulated" [Zakeri Begum vs. Sakina Begum (1892) 19 I.A. 157, 165, 19 Cal. 689]. Yet bargaining is very much present over the amount of *mahr*. Sometimes, such bargaining leads to unpleasant occurrences and cancellation of marriage. The girl's parents always desire to fix a high amount which ought to be beyond the means of the bridegroom so that their daughter will not have to face the threat of divorce from her husband in future.

The fixed amount is either deferred only, or is handed over immediately, or paid in cash or in kind. Though 40 per cent *mahr* is payably at the time of marriage, only two incidents of such payment had been referred to in our present study. It is usually asserted that the *mahr* money is a good security for the woman in case of any difficulties in her marital life, and when she is divorced the *mahr* money has to be given to her. But if the divorce has occurred due to her own fault, she is not entitled to the *mahr* money. Otherwise, the woman is also entitled to get her *mahr* after her husband's death to be paid by her sons. In case the woman dies before the husband, then her father and brothers can demand the *mahr* money from her husband.[9]

After the ceremony is over, the sweets brought by the bridegroom's party are distributed among the people who are present at the ceremony. Then in the evening the 'face viewing ceremony' takes place where both the bride and the bridegroom see each other. This ritual customarily takes place in the verandah of the house, where elderly women treat the bridegroom with home made sweets. It is followed by some folk practices which vary from village to village, from locality to locality. Here gifts are offered to the bridegroom by the parents, elders and close relatives. These gifts include wristwatch, rings and sometimes even cash.

Later, on the same day, the bride is escorted to her husband's house along with some maid servants or such women with whom she is on easy terms. After two days, the daughter along with her husband comes back to her parents house, and stays there for seven days, which is usually called *astamangla* in Bengali. But there is no hard and fast rule that the bridegroom must stay for seven days. The usual practice is to stay there for two or three days. And after *astamangla*, the wife is escorted by some close relatives of the bridegroom's family along with her husband. And thereby she becomes a member of her husband's family.

Divorce

As far as the practice of divorce among Bengali Muslims is concerned, the survey reveals that Muslim women have to face the practice of arbitrary divorce. But there is nothing to deny that religion plays a vital role in this regard; in the practice of divorce or *talaq*, religion is one of the important factors. The occurrence of divorce has a strong correlation with other social and economic variables.

A divorce or separation is usually not the result of a sudden, isolated case of friction between the husband and wife. It is usually a result of a series of developments and there is frequently (according to our survey) a specific reason behind the occurrence of divorce/separation of Muslim women.

According to the survey, there are 36 divorce cases in the district of Murshidabad and 31 divorce cases in Barddhaman district. If we take note of the reasons behind the divorce then we find that there is a great divergence between theory and practice on the question of divorce among the Bengali Muslims. In our study, we have found that no husband waited for three menstrual cycles for the final pronouncement of *talaq*, though the

Quran has been very specific and clear on the subject. In this regard Levy[10] rightly observes:

> When family life is concerned, in marriage, divorce and the distribution of inheritance, the provisions of the *sha'r* would appear to be very widely neglected.

The gap between theory and practice is also very evident on the questions of the grounds for divorce. In our study, we found that the reasons for divorce were varied. Extra-marital relationship of the husbands, poor economic conditions of both the parties and family quarrels are the most prominent. Other reasons behind divorce are: dowry; no issue; second marriage; and a re-established relationship with the first wife. In two cases, respondents were divorced due to their sexual inability to give birth to children which occurred after a long period of marriage. Another reason cited behind divorce was the husband's absence for years togethers from the wife's side.

It is interesting to note that 6.25 per cent cases in both the districts, Murshidabad and Barddhaman, the *Quranic* prescription regarding divorce had been followed (see Table 5.5). If we take note of our study then we find that in one case divorce had taken place in the presence of the *qazi* in the *gram panchayat* of Murshidabad district and in seven cases in Barddhaman. Most of the divorce cases have occurred in the presence of the local people. And these local people usually are not aware of the *Quranic* principles of *talaq*. They are only interested in getting back the goods and money which the respondent's parents had given to their son-in-law as dowry.

It was also found that when a divorce had occurred in the presence of local people no respondent was present there and no prior consent had been taken from them. Sometimes divorce had taken place against the will of the respondents. In one case, divorce notice was given through mail. Eighteen respondents mentioned that their divorce had occurred in the court. Here it is to be noted that some of the husbands moved the court and informed the respondents by mail that they had been divorced.

Table 5.5
Occurrence of Talaq

In presence of	*Murshidabad*		*Barddhaman*		*Total*	
	n	%	*n*	%	*n*	%
Qazi	01	1.72	07	10.00	08	6.25
Local people	26	44.84	18	25.71	44	34.38
In court	10	17.24	08	11.43	18	14.06
By mail	01	1.72	00	00.00	01	0.78
None	02	3.45	00	00.00	02	1.56
N.A.	18	31.03	37	52.86	55	42.97
Total	58	100.00	70	100.00	128	100.00

Only in one case was divorce sought by the respondent's family due to her husband's regular involvement in anti-social activities. But in most cases, the respondent's family or the respondent herself was not aware or rather not interested in the *Quranic* rules to be followed on the question of divorce. Ignorance of the respondents and respondents' families had been fully utilized by the husbands.

From the above discussion, we may conclude that divorced/separated Muslim women in West Bengal are leading a miserable life. Their general condition is very pathetic. Those who cite the example of *mahr* as case of maintenance, they are in reality trying to give us a wrong picture about the position of Muslim women. In our survey we have found that the Muslim law is fettered with inequalities, the women in every case being less equal than men. Divorced and separated Muslim women have not only been oppressed by the patriarchal bias of the society, but they are additionally exploited by the unavailability of any legal protection. It is interesting to note that some respondents' husbands moved the court and then informed the respondents that they had been divorced.

Razia Patil[11] has vividly explained the practice of divorce which is common in all parts of the country. She argues that:

> One of our neighbours divorced his wife by pronouncing *talaq*. She had an infant in her arms and she herself was only 18 or 19 years old. She had no parents. Her only aunt was not ready to take her back in her home. In spite of her tears and her pleas to her husband not to pronounce *talaq*, the divorce took place and the poor girl was literally thrown out on the streets.

So, any attempt at betterment of the position and status of divorced and separated Muslim women in West Bengal demands positive attacks on poverty and on socio-religious restrictions which presuppose male superiority and dominance.

Notes

1. Reuban Levy (1962): *The Structure of Islam*, Cambridge: Cambridge University Press, p. 242.
2. H. Hidayatullah (1972): *Mulla's Principles of Mahomedan Law*, Bombay: N.M. Tripathi Private Limited, p. xxiii.
3. A.M.A. Shushtery (1972): *Outlines of Islamic Culture*, Bangalore: The Bangalore Printing and Publishing Company Limited, p. 397.
4. Ibid, p. 424.
5. Asghar Ali Engineer (1992): *The Rights of Women in Islam*, New Delhi: Sterling Publishers Private Limited, p. 108.
6. Ahmad Muhammad al-Haufi(1954): *Al Mar 'ah fial-sh 'ar al-Jahili*, Cairo, p. 151.
7. Asghar Ali Engineer (1992): op. cit., p. 55.
8. *The Quran*: Shrah 4,4.

9. Shibani Roy (1979): *Status of Muslim Women in North India*, Delhi: B.R. Publishing Corporation, p. 83.
10. Reuban Levy (1962): op. cit.
11. Razia Patel (1995): "Problems of Muslim Women" in Asghar Ali Engineer (ed.): *Problems of Muslim Women in India*, Bombay: Orient Longman, p. 175.

118B

6

Practice of *Purdah*

In many countries of the world and especially in Islamic countries the practice of *purdah* has been widely prevalent among the Muslims for more than 1,000 years. Feminine veiling and seclusion are referred to as *purdah*, derived from the Persian word denoting '*curtain*'. In its general meaning, it is an Islamic custom ordained by *Allah* for women. As per the *Quran*, *purdah* means "casting down one's looks" and "guarding one's private parts" and "avoiding display of a woman's beauty to any other than her husband or his very near and dear ones."

The practice of *purdah* evolved gradually during the first three centuries of Islam and established itself firmly during the tenth and eleventh centuries, sanctioned by the interpretation of the influential theologians of Abbasid Caliphate.

According to Engineer[1]:

The custom of veiling (*purdah*) began during the Umayyad period. A critical evaluation of the Prophet's time would clearly show that women used to pray in mosques with their faces uncovered and hands open and interacted with the Prophet and his male companions in religious and other matters. Later, when foreign influences, specially of Rome and Persia, appeared on the scene, women came under increasing restrictions. The rulers began to maintain large harems which needed to be strictly guarded from outsiders. Soon the ways of the rulers began to be followed by other members of the ruling classes and, finally, by the people in general. Thus *purdah* became common. Slowly, women were even ever forbidden from attending mosques for public prayers.

In this regard, Shushtery[2] observes:

During the lifetime of the Prophet and during the period of his first four successors, the Umayyed and Abbaside Khalif, women freely mixed with men and some high class ladies, such as Ayesha, daughter of Talha, even declined to wear the veil. The practice, however, gradually spread in its intensity according to the circumstances of the age, till it reached the present intolerable position. Strict *purdah* system probably became popular after the fall of Baghdad and the rise of Moghuls and the Timurids in Iran and India. During this period, partly owing to the inclination of the Moghal rulers and partly owing to the insistence of the orthodox section, who became very powerful and laid emphasis on the complete seclusion of women, the present *purdah* system became effective.

The practice of *purdah* has become an extreme form of male dominance. It has been practised by excluding women from all types of activities outside home by secluding them from all men, except close male relatives. *Purdah* denies women the freedom of action and participation in economic and social life. It divides the whole social life into two strictly separate and exclusive spheres---the outdoor life of the men and the other, the indoor secluded life of the women. They are confined to their houses and if they go out of their houses, they must put on a *burqa* (a head to foot cloak) or a *chaddar* (a sheet, to wrap the body in) in order to veil themselves from the men outside, so as to prevent any likelihood of contact with them. They cover not only their body but also their faces. These prejudices originated in the feudal era wherein the ruling Muslim classes wanted to protect their womenfolk from others and so kept them under strict seclusion. However, that tradition was given Islamic legitimacy along with such traditions that required women to observe *purdah* even in the presence of a blind man.

There is a wide variation in observing *purdah* in Muslim countries. No uniform agreement is there among the theologians as to which ornament should be concealed by a woman when she is in *purdah*. In countries like Turkey, Egypt, Iran, Iraq and Syria, women could go out with a cloak over their heads, reaching just below the knees. In Arabia, even men used to cover their faces when they considered that they would be exposed to evil glances. Regarding the practice of *purdah* in India, Shushtery[3] observes:

> It is said that when Emperor Timur invaded India and captured Delhi, he issued an order prohibiting Muslim women from showing themselves to strangers and directed them to travel in covered conveyances. If the story is true, it suggests that strict *purdah* had not been enforced till then in India, at least among Indian born Muslim women.

The *Quran* enjoined the faithful to keep their women well covered and to give them a distinguishing mark so that they would be recognized and not be bothered. *Quranic* prescriptions are often cited by devout Muslims as the basis for the observance of *purdah* by Muslim women, and some of the Prophet's recorded words seem to have recommended some limitations on women's activities and dress. The *Quranic* principles regarding *purdah* are as follows:

> *Surah 24, 31*
> Tell the believing women to lower their eyes, guard their private parts, and not display their charms except what is apparent out-

wardly, and cover their bosoms with their veils and not to show their finery except to their husbands or their fathers or fathers-in-law, their sons or step-sons, brothers, or their brothers' and sisters' sons, or their women attendants or captives, or male attendants who do not have any need (for women), or boys not yet conscious of sex. They should not walk stamping their feet lest they make known what they hide of their ornaments. O believers, turn to *Allah*, every one of you. So that you may find success.

Surah 24, 60

As for your women past the age of bearing children, who have no hope of marriage, there is no harm if they take off their outer garments, but in such a way that they do not display their charms; yet if they avoid this it would be better for them. *Allah* is all-hearing and all-knowing.

Surah 33, 33

Stay at home, and do not deck yourselves with ostentation as in the days of paganism; fulfill your devotional obligations, pay the *zakat*, and obey *Allah* and His Apostle. *Allah* desires to remove impurities from you, O inmates of this house, and to cleanse and bring out the best in you.

Surah 33, 53

O you who believe, do not enter the house of the Prophet for a meal without awaiting the proper time, unless asked, and enter when you are invited, and depart when you have eaten, and do not stay on talking. This puts the Prophet to inconvenience, and he feals embarrassed before you; but *Allah* is not embarrassed in (saying) the truth. And when you ask his wife for something of utility, ask for it from behind the screen. This is for the purity of your hearts and theirs. It does not behove you to trouble the Prophet, or to ever marry his wives after him. This would indeed be serious in the sight of *Allah*.

Surah 33, 59

O Prophet, tell your wives and daughters, and the women of the faithful, to draw their wraps a little over their faces. They will

> thus be recognised and no harm will come to them. *Allah* is forgiving and kind.

Regarding *purdah,* the pronouncements of the Prophet are as follows: Hazrat Jarir says, "I asked the Holy Prophet what I should do if I happen to cast a look by chance." The Holy Prophet replied, "Turn your eyes away" (*Abu Da'ud*).

According to Hazrat Buraidah, the Holy Prophet told Hazrat Ali 'not to cast a second look', for the first look was pardonable but the second was prohibited' (*Abu Da'ud*).

> "On the Day of Judgement, molten lead will be poured into the eyes of the man who looks at the charms of a woman lustfully (*Takmalah. Fath-al-Qadir*).

These relevant *Quranic* passages, however, are somewhat ambiguous and do not prescribe in details the ideal features of a woman's dress and behaviour. Indeed, Muslim women observe *purdah* in a variety of ways in South Asia and throughout the world, and some Muslim women do not observe *purdah* at all.[4]

We are also to remember that *purdah* or *purdah*-like behaviour are not restricted to Muslim women alone. Doranne Jacobson[5] opines:

> There is evidence that women were veiled and secluded among various pre-Islamic Mediterranean, Arab and Persian peoples, and in recent centuries many Hindu, Christian, Buddhist, and other women of various religions of the globe have traditionally followed practices that closely resemble Muslim *purdah* observances in important respects. Therefore, on the basis of Islamic scriptures alone, it is difficult to explain or understand *purdah* in its many forms.

With the rising tide of modernism and sexual equality among the Muslim people, with the consequent proposals for legal abolition of *purdah* or its gradual disappearance from among the Muslims, the advocates of *purdah,* especially among the *ulema*, have defended it on various grounds. The arguments which they have raised are rather superficial and without any scientific undertones. Maulana Jalal-Ud-Din Ansar Umri defends the *purdah* on the plea that men and women are like fire and cotton whose meeting together is always destructive. In Maulana Umri's view, it has neither sense nor reason to merit consideration. He would not realise that in spite of the differences, both men and women are 'sheep of the same flock'.

Other advocates of *purdah* system are Allama Farid Vajadi, a well known Egyptian scholar and the Pakistani politico-religious leader, Maulana Abdul Ala Maududi. Allama Vajadi based his defence of the segregation of the sexes on the observations and conclusions of modern sciences, in particular of biology and sociology.

On the other hand, Maulana Maududi branded women as tragic beings. The functions of her body, such as menstruation, pregnancy and child suckling and rearing, make her physiologically unfit for any work or activity except that of bearing children and performing housekeeping chores. To the contrary, man has no such biological disabilities and burdens. To Maududi, man's biological role in procreation is very brief and free from all responsibilities.

As Maududi[6] puts it:

> In the matter of continuation of the race, men has been entrusted with no other task except that of sowing the seeds. Afterwards, he is absolutely free to do whatever he likes in any walk of life. As against this, the whole burden (of procreation) has been put upon the woman, for the performance of which she is prepared from the time she was a mere foetus in the womb of her mother.

Such differentiation of Maulana Maudidi makes man an active partner and woman a passive one. It is for the smooth running of society that the two partners must be allocated those sphere of activities and functions for which they are fit on the basis of their bodily and mental capabilities. To him, the *purdah* is, therefore, a necessary mode of organizing human social life, activities and functions on this basis. This is nothing but the *purdah* theory of dichotomous parallelism in sex and society of Allama Vajadi and Maulana Maududi.

Maulana Maududi[7] further declares:

> This is the division of work which Nature itself has made between the two sexes of mankind. Biology, physiology, psychology and all the branches of social sciences indicate this division. A good (*saleh*) civilization is one which accepts this dispensing of Nature as it is. Once it is done, you may give woman her proper place, give her honour in the society, respect her, give her justifiable cultural and social rights, but burden her only with domestic duties, while all outdoor responsibilities and the command of the family to man.

He also warns those who would attempt to do otherwise. He observes:

> Any civilization, which will try to efface this division, may achieve, for some time, a measure of progress, glory and splendour, but is bound to bring ruin upon itself in the end. The reason is that when women are loaded like men with the same cultural and social responsibilities and tasks, they will inevitably cast away their natural functions. Such in the destruction of humanity itself.

The *purdah* system is based on these ideas and beliefs that sex is a dichotomous phenomenon, with absolute differences between the two sexes, found both in their anatomy, physiology and psychology, which makes them fundamentally unlike each other.

On the other hand, observers of *purdah* claim certain advantages of it. It is suggested that Muslim women, remaining strangers to the society of men, can exclusively attend to the work of the household and can give sufficient time for the children. Then, they have also observed that they may mix with members of their own sex and enjoy their company without suspicions being raised on the part of their husbands and their husbands may freely interplay the society of their own sex without being suspected or misunderstood by their wives.

Now the question is, can we draw such a boundary between the two sexes? If it is so, then why the practice of *purdah* was unknown to Muslims for such a long period of time in the history of Islam? Some scholars are categorical that the practice of *purdah* was not there until the third century of the *hizra*. In this regard, Reuban Levy quotes Tabari[8] to show that until the third century of the *hizra*, and even later, women used to pray in mosques along with men. The face, hands and upper side of the feet did not need to be covered, though there is some controversy about the last detail.[9]

Regarding *purdah*, Ibn Batuta[10] observes:

> Their women showed no modesty in the presence of men and did not veil. Yet they were assiduous in their prayers. Anyone who wished to marry them could do so, but they would not go on a journey with their husband. Even if one of them wished it her kinsfolk would prevent her. The women there have friends and companions amongst men who are not related to them. So also the men have friends amongst men who are not related to them. A man may enter his house and find his wife with her friend and yet will not disapprove.

But with the passage of time, the advent of modern education and awakening and with the rise of scientific outlook among the Muslims, the problem of *purdah* and Muslim women has arisen in one form or other. The utility of the practice has been put into question. Its very existence has been challenged even in some Muslim countries. Modernist reform movements took roots in many Islamic countries and ultimately culminated in the Kamalist revolution in modern Turkey, when *purdah* was discarded and polygamy abolished.[11]

Against this general background, we are to analyze the observance of *purdah* in our field area among the divorced/separated Muslim women in West Bengal. Here, the concept of modesty (*laj/saram*) is central to the ideology of *purdah* as well as to all other rules governing women's dress and behaviour. Female modesty as it is conceived of in both Murshidabad and Barddhaman is similar in many respects to other parts of West Bengal as well as India. The Bengali Muslim women generally keep their heads covered with the *sari* in public, in front of respected elders, in front of outsiders and during prayers. In a Bengali *mian* (gentleman) Muslim family, women observe *purdah* by remaining inside their houses, by veiling their faces with the *sari* whenever they do go outside their home; with some wearing the *burqa* whenever they move out of their home. The particular details of the manner in which *purdah* is observed vary among different families and socio-economic groups. The *purdah* practices of the high class Bengali Muslim groups are different in many respects from those of the lower socio-economic groups.

In general, there is a tendency to observe *purdah* among the Bengali Muslim women whatever may be their socio-economic position. Regarding the practice of *purdah* in both the districts under review, women in *purdah* normally do not allow themselves to be seen by men who are not their relatives or *kutumba* (affinities). Women in *bhadrolok* (gentleman) or 'well-to-do-gentlemen' families used to appear before their fathers, brothers, husbands, uncles, cousins as well as close male affinies, such as sons-in-law, brothers-in-law and fathers-in-law without the *burqa*.

Regarding the observance of *purdah* the respondents were asked a few relevant and related questions. In our study we found that a majority of the Bengali Muslim women engage themselves in indoor activities though sometimes they move out when needed. They were asked: "Do you think Muslim women must confine themselves in their homes?" Out of total 128 respondents 89.84 per cent answered in favour of it and 10.16 per cent answered in the negative. And among 89.84 per cent of those who favoured, the percentages of Murshidabad and Barddhaman are 94.83 per cent and 85.71 per cent, respectively (see Table 6.1).

Table 6.1

Respondents' Attitudes Towards their Confinement

Districts	*Be confined*		*Do not be confined*		*Total*	
	n	%	*n*	%	*n*	%
Murshidabad	55	94.83	03	5.17	58	100.00
Barddhaman	60	85.71	10	14.29	70	100.00
Total	115	89.84	13	10.16	128	100.00

If we take note of the use of *burqa*, then we find that out of the 128 respondents, 85.94 per cent women do not use the *burqa* and 14.06 per cent respondents wear it. If we look at Table 6.2 we find that the percentage of Murshidabad (94.83%) in this respect is higher than the district of Barddhaman (78.57%). Though, in general, the majority do not wear *burqa*, the practice of veil has a presence among them; 14.06 per cent respondents of both the districts use veil in presence of outsiders, 75.78 per cent always use it. In Murshidabad, 20.69 per cent use it in the presence of elderly people, 8.62 per cent in the presence of outsiders and 68.97 per cent wear the veil all the time. In Barddhaman, 8.57 per cent use the veil in presence of outsiders and 81.43 per cent always use it. This goes to show that the use of the veil is very common in both the districts of Murshidabad and Barddhaman (see Tables 6.2 and 6.3).

Table 6.2
Use of Burqa among the Respondents

Districts	*Use*		*Don't Use*		*Total*	
	n	%	*n*	%	*n*	%
Murshidabad	03	5.17	55	94.83	58	100.00
Barddhaman	15	21.43	55	78.57	70	100.00
Total	18	14.06	110	85.94	128	100.00

Table 6.3
Number and Percentage of Respondents Who Use Veil (in presence of the following persons)

District	*In Presence of Elderly People*		*In Presence of Outsiders*		*Always*		*Don't Use*		*Total*	
	n	%	*n*	%	*n*	%	*n*	%	*n*	%
Murshidabad	12	20.69	05	8.62	40	68.97	01	1.72	58	100.00
Barddhaman	06	8.57	06	8.57	57	81.43	01	1.43	70	100.00
Total	18	14.06	11	8.60	97	75.78	02	1.57	128	100.00

Parents also show a strong attitude towards the observance of *purdah*. In Table 6.4, we find that 29 respondents in both the districts have no guardians. Out of a total 99 guardians, 64.06 per cent support the observance of *purdah* and 13.28 per cent do not support it.

In order to trace the reasons behind the observance of *purdah*, we find that in Murshidabad, 60.34 per cent parents support it because the Muslim *Shari'a* lays it down, 3.45 per cent for status and 17.24 per cent parents do not support it at all. In Barddhaman, 35.71 per cent support the practice of *purdah* as the *Shari'a* demands it, 11.43 per cent for safety; 14.29 per cent for family status, 10 per cent do not support it at all and

Table 6.4

Parents' Attitude Towards the Custom of Purdah

Districts	*Support*		*Don't Support*		*N.A.*		*Total*	
	n	*%*	*n*	*%*	*n*	*%*	*n*	*%*
Murshidabad	37	63.79	10	17.24	11	18.97	58	100.00
Barddhaman	45	64.29	07	10.00	18	25.71	70	100.00
Total	82	64.06	17	13.28	29	29.66	128	100.00

2.86 per cent cannot cite the reasons behind the observance of *purdah*. On the other hand, in both the districts it is found that 46.88 per cent observe *purdah* for Muslim *Shari'a*; 6.25 per cent for safety; 9.37 per cent for status and 13.28 per cent do not support it (see Table 6.5). As far as free movement of the Muslim women in those two districts is concerned, most of the Bengali Muslim women do refrain from casual strolls around the village, and they leave their villages only to visit relatives, to attend important family functions such as a wedding or to visit hospital. If we take note of Table 6.6, we find that 4.69 per cent normally move about and 90.62 per cent, when needed. But 4.69 per cent do not move out at all. In Murshidabad, none move out of their homes whereas in Barddhaman, 8.57 per cent

Table 6.5

Reasons Behind the Support of Purdah as Revealed by the Parents

Districts	*For Muslim Shari'a*		*For Safety*		*For Status*		*Don't Support*		*Can't Say*		*No Guardians*		*Total*	
	n	*%*	*n*	*%*	*n*	*%*	*N*	*%*	*N*	*%*	*N*	*%*	*N*	*%*
Murshidabad	35	60.34	00	00	02	3.45	10	17.24	00	00	11	18.97	58	100.00
Barddhaman	25	35.71	08	11.43	10	14.29	07	10.00	02	2.86	18	25.71	70	100.00
Total	60	46.88	08	6.25	12	9.37	17	13.28	02	1.56	29	22.66	128	100.00

move about usually. But in Murshidabad, 96.55 per cent move when needed and 85.72 per cent in Barddhaman move at the time of need.

Table 6.6

Respondents' Movement Outside their Homes

Districts	*Move Out*		*When Needed*		*Not at All*		*Total*	
	n	%	*n*	%	*n*	%	*n*	%
Murshidabad	00	0.0	56	96.55	02	3.45	58	100.00
Barddhaman	06	8.57	60	85.72	04	5.71	70	100.00
Total	06	4.69	116	90.62	06	4.69	128	100.00

Indeed, it is equally relevant to analyze parents' willingness to allow their daughters to work somewhere and their attitude towards the place of work. Out of 99 respondents, 72.73 per cent showed positive attitude towards allowing their daughters to work somewhere and 27.27 percent answered negatively. In Murshidabad among 47 respondents 72.34 per cent answered in the positive and 27.66 per cent answered in the negative. On the whole, parents' attitude towards the place of work of their daughters run as follows: out of a total 99 respondents, 32.32 per cent favoured allowing their daughter to work outside home and 43.44 per cent inside home. In Murshidabad, out of a total 47 respondents 10.64 per cent favoured allowing their daughters to work outside home. In Barddhaman, 51.92 per cent favoured allowing their daughters to work outside home and 26.92 per cent inside home (see Tables 6.7 and 6.8).

If we endorse the view that the practice of *purdah* with all its connotations is against the canons of human progress toward a society that offers equal opportunity to every human being and discourages suppression—whether material or spiritual—then we must consider the district of Barddhaman to be significantly more progressive than the district of Murshidabad. Of course, making such sweeping generalizations seems to be rather hazardous; so we hasten to temper our observation with

Table 6.7

Parents' Willingness to Allow their Daughters to Work

Districts	*Positive*		*Negative*		*Total*	
	n	%	*n*	%	*n*	%
Murshidabad	34	72.34	13	27.66	47	100.00
Barddhaman	38	73.08	14	26.92	52	100.00
Total	72	72.73	27	27.27	99	100.00

Table 6.8

Parents' Attitude Towards their Daughters' Place of Work

Districts	*Outside Home*		*Inside Home*		*N.A.*		*Total*	
	n	%	*n*	%	*n*	%	*n*	%
Murshidabad	05	10.64	29	61.70	13	27.66	47	100.00
Barddhaman	27	51.92	14	26.92	11	21.16	52	100.00
Total	32	32.32	43	43.44	24	24.24	99	100.00

the question "as could be discerned from an inspection of the narrow ambit of a vast social canvas on which our survey could throw some light". This can be justified by the following pieces of statistics:

---- Parents in Barddhaman are far more willing to let their daughters work outside their homes (nearly 52% as against 10% in Murshidabad).

---- More than 9 per cent of the interviewed women actually move freely outside their homes when there is no urgent need to do so. However, not a single respondent in Murshidabad was found to possess this liberty.

---- Nearly 95 per cent of the women interviewed in Murshidabad support their own confinement, while the corresponding figure in Barddhaman is lower, i.e., 85 per cent.

— Finally, 60 per cent of the interviewees of Murshidabad support the practice of *purdah* because of their reverence to Muslim *Sharia*, but in Barddhaman, only 35 per cent do so for purely religious reasons and 11 per cent practise *purdah* for safety.

In both the *gram panchayats*, it was noticed that *purdah* really is an institution of the middle and upper section divorced and separated Bengali Muslim women, confined mainly, even exclusively, to the elite classes and sections of Muslim society. *Purdah* is not observed or practised by all classes and sections for reasons of poverty and economic hardships. The poorer sections of the Bengali Muslim people cannot keep their womenfolk strictly confined within the home, because they have to go out to work and earn a livelihood. Many of the divorced and separated Bengali Muslim women have to seek domestic service in better-off houses of their locality. So they cannot confine themselves to their houses or go out with a *burqa* on.

In this regard Shustery[12] opines:

> *Purdah* is essentially a social problem and it is bound to be decided by social needs and necessities. At present; the Indian custom is restricted more to the middle classes than to the richer or the poorer. The villagers and poorer classes are, to a great extent free, and the rich can afford to remain secluded in their big houses or to enjoy fresh air in motor cars. Some of them are in different circumstances, specially those who have received western education. It is the middle classes, possessing neither big houses nor suitable conveyances, that suffer under the existing practice. They will probably give the lead in the matter and thus help to do away with a custom which has over-stayed its utility. That the *purdah* has had little effect on the progress of women is perhaps inferable from the great women poetesses and administrators that Islam has produced.

But it is equally true that among the low status Bengali

Muslims, *purdah* continues to be considered as a mark of prestige and is not being abandoned. People who were in the lower order imitated the higher and the result was the prevailing seclusion of women in Bengal, which has excluded them from taking part in the performance of many useful tasks both for themselves and the society. *Purdah* has become a symbol of upward mobility rather than horizontal solidarity because the new entrants into its ranks savoured it more than those to whom it came as a matter of course. They cherished it, assiduously guarding against the smallest crack in the façade. Some of the poor Bengali Muslims, who have become more prosperous, would probably tend to observe *purdah*, as in fact has happened in a few families. Certainly, none of the poor Muslims want to give up *purdah* because it is "outdated and useless"; quite the reverse is true. So it was, and still is, that the lower professional classes such as butchers and petty shopkeepers and who bettered their lot through agriculture keep their women much more rigidly than the upper classes.[13]

Rokeya[14] has narrated an unbelievable incident that occurred during the first half of this century. From it we get a clear idea about how strictly women used to observe *purdah*. Accompanied by a maid-servant and veiled with a heavy *burqa*, an upper class woman, a relative of Rokeya, was boarding a train at Kiul station. She accidentally fell down in the space between the train and the platform. The maid-servant pulled her by the *burqa*. But the *burqa* was torn and the woman was unable to rise. Some porters present there offered to help, but the maid-servant would not allow them to do so. The train was due to leave. However, it waited for half an hour and at last it ran over her. This is nothing but a cruel example of seclusion.

It is to be noted that womenfolk of the labourers and those doing menial jobs, were an integral part of the labour force. For them, the ultimate goal in economic achievement was to be able to retreat to the shelter of the home and not be forced to toil at their demeaning occupation. As soon as male members like fathers, husbands, or sons could afford, they resigned from the activity of the outside world, retreating behind the curtain and in this way they came to be called "*bibi*"(gentle-lady).

From our above discussion we may conclude that the tragedy of Muslim women, as propounded by *purdah* ideologists, is not in reality biological; it is rather socio-economical and contextual. There is no law of nature which makes women inferior and subordinate to man. But innumerable customs, taboos, beliefs, prejudices, superstitions, laws and institutions make them socially inferior and economically dependent on man. Further, seclusion and isolation have forced the Bengali Muslim women in general into a sad plight; divorced and separated Bengali Muslim women have been forced into a limited circle of interaction, which has denied them the opportunity to function as mature and confident human beings. There is nothing in the biology and physiology of the female sex which makes her inferior, but there is much in the experiences of her childhood and adult life, that she has lived in the *purdah* within her social and cultural environment, which makes her so. It has rendered the divorced and separated Bengali Muslim woman incapable of contributing to a lot of activities which are suited to her interests and talents. It is the kind of family life, neighbourhood, and the kind of social climate of opinions, inhibitions and restrictions in which she lives that makes her inferior and dependent on man. In concrete terms, it is the *purdah* ideology and society which makes the Bengali Muslim women so inferior and subordinate to men. And, indeed, one may go to the extent of suggesting that a major factor of the commonly backward socio-economic condition of the Bengali Muslim women is *purdah*.

Notes

1. Asghar Ali Engineer (1992): *The Rights of Women in Islam*, Sterling Publishers Pvt. Ltd. New Delhi, p.91.
2. A.M.A. Shushtery (1953): *Outlines of Islamic Culture*, The Bangalore Printing and Publishing Co. Ltd., Bangalore, p.421.
3. Ibid, p.422.
4. Leela Dube with Abdul Rahman Kutty (1969): *Matriliny and Islam: Religion and Society in Laccadives* University of Sagar Monograph in Anthropology and Sociology, National Publishing House, Delhi, p.24.
5. Dorannc Jacobson (1976): "The Veil of Virtue: Purdah and Muslim Family in the Bhopal Region of Central India" in Imtiaz Ahmad (ed.), *Family, Kinship and Marriage among Muslims in India*, Monohar, New Delhi, p. 171.
6. Abdul Ala Maududi: Quoted by Mazhar ul Haq Khan in *Purdah and Polygamy*, p.22.
7. Ibid.
8. Tabari Vol.I p. 2469: Quoted by Reuban Levy (1962): *Social Structure of Islam*, Cambridge University Press, Cambridge. p.126.
9. Reuban Levy, Ibid, p.126.
10. Ibid, p.127.
11. Mazhar Ul Haq Khan (1982): *Purdah and Polygamy*, Amar Prakashan, Delhi, p.18.
12. A.M.A. Shushtery: op.cit., p.423.
13. Jamila Brijbhushan (1980): *Muslim Women: In Purdah and Out of It*. Vikas Publishing House Pvt. Ltd., Delhi, p.21.
14. Quoted by Ghulam Murshid (1983): *Reluctant Debutante: Response of Bengali Women to Modernization 1849-1905*, from *Rokeya Ranchanabali* (in Bengali), Rajshahi, p.482.

7

Conclusion

We shall now analyse the present position of the divorced and separated Bengali Muslim women in the light of our hypotheses. Our first hypothesis is that divorce of Muslim women is more prevalent among the low income group and low status group Muslim people. On the basis of cost of living index constructed for the agricultural labourer, which can be assumed to be relevant for all rural people, the poverty line in West Bengal has been calculated at Rs. 170.40 per month per person. However, we shall not confine ourselves to this definition and consider all households having monthly income of Rs. 600 and less as low income households.

The main reason for this is that a monthly income of Rs. 600 for a household with an average size of five persons, yields a per capita income of Rs. 120. Thus, our cut-off point (Rs. 120 per capita) lies below the line constructed by Minhas.[1] As a result, we can be reasonably sure that households having income levels of Rs. 600 per month can be considered lying below the poverty line.

With this definition in mind, we see that, of the interviewed families, at least 77 per cent in Murshidabad and 57 per cent in Barddhaman belong to the low income group. It is to be noted that the data was obtained after interviewing all the divorced/separated Muslim women in the villages under survey. Hence, the question of omittance of any 'rich' or 'middle' class divorced/separated women in the survey process does not arise, and the data can be said to provide the complete picture of the relationship between divorce and income levels in the selected areas. Let us then test the above hypothesis (under the assumption that a ratio of 55 per cent and above can be deemed to indicate a clear majority— represented in our hypothesis by the objective 'more') as well as compare the incidents of divorce in the two districts.

Let P_1 be the proportion of low income divorced/separated Muslim women in Murshidabad and P_2 be the corresponding ratio in Barddhaman as indicated by us. We shall test

(a) the hypothesis that $P_1 \geq 55\%$,

(b) the hypothesis that $P_2 \geq 55\%$, and

(c) the null hypothesis that $P_1 = P_2$.

Where P_1 and P_2 represent the said ratio for the two districts respectively—in statistical terminology, we call them population parameters.

Now, $P_1 = 0.775$ and

$P_2 = 0.571$

Under the Null hypothesis C, the equal but unknown proportion for both districts (b) is:

$P = 0.664$.

Expected value of P_1-P_2 is 0, and

S.E. (Standard Error) of P_1—P_2 = 0.0838713.

$\therefore$ Z = 2.432298.

Since the alternative hypothesis of (c) is $P_1 \neq P_2$, the value of Z does not fall in the critical region $|Z| \geq 2.58$, it is not significant at 1 per cent level. But it is significant at 5 per cent level. So there is sufficient reason to doubt the authenticity of Null hypothesis (c), i.e., the equality of relationship between income and the practice of divorce in the two districts.

Now, to test (a); we test

Ho: $P_1 \geq 0.55$ (where P = population proportion)

against H_1: $P_1 < 0.55$.

$\therefore$ observed $P_1 = 0.775$; while if Ho is true,

expected value is 0.55

So standard error of $P_1 = 0.653238$

hence, our $Z_1 = 3.44$.

Since the value of Z_1, i.e. 3.44 (approx.) exceeds---1.645, or in other words falls in the region $Z \geq 1.645$, we accept Hypothesis at 5 per cent level of significance. So, we conclude that, in Murshidabad, divorce is more prevalent among the low income group.

To test (b), we find that

Ho: $P_2 \geq 0.55$ against H_1: $P_2 < 0.55$.

Following the same process, we get the value for the observed $P_1 = 0.571$, and the expected value equal to 0.55, with the result that the

(Standard error of P_2) = 0.0594617

Hence $Z_2 = 0.35316$.

We accept the hypothesis at 5 per cent level of significance, i.e. in Barddhaman too, it can be concluded that divorce is more prevalent among the low income group.

Status is not a clearly definable term. By status, Linton[2] meant a position in social system occupied by designated individuals; by role, the behavioural enacting of the patterned expectations attributed to that position. According to Merton

(1957: 369-70), the social status of an individual is his status set, each of the statuses in turn having their distinctive role set. Role set to him is the complement of role relationships which persons have by virtue of occupying a particular social status.

Status tries to depict the social standing of people. But we should remember that social standards can vary significantly in intertemporal and interspatial terms. Further, it depends on who is looking at whom. To a rickshaw-puller, a taxi driver may appear to be belonging to a higher strata, though the latter may be just another 'cabbie' to the person sitting inside his taxi. Indeed as Galsworth wrote, "there is no view except from a viewpoint ..." Therefore, we shall first identify the professions, which allegedly make a person belong to a 'low-status' group.

We include menial professions like those of a day-labourer, rickshaw-puller, gardener and *bidi*-maker in the 'low-status' category. To be more specific, jobs which need little or no formal training, or which involve mostly raw physical labour, or which offer little remuneration, or a combination of the above can be treated as wreckers of social prestige. With this view in mind, we can easily exclude service holders, wholesalers, students, masons for the purpose of establishing the relationship specified in our hypothesis. Further, we also omit people listed under the head 'agriculture' (excluding agricultural labourer) because cultivation certainly does not relegate somebody to the lower rung of a social ladder in a rural area.

Against the above mentioned backdrop, we find that 45 per cent (approx.) of the husbands (of the divorced/separated women covered in our survey) in Murshidabad---26 out of 58 to be exact--- belong to the low status category (as defined by us). The corresponding figure in Barddhaman is 54 per cent (38 out of 70). We can try a little mathematical exercise at this juncture.

We form the following hypothesis:

(a) Ho: $P_1 \geq 55\%$ against H_1: $P_1 < 55\%$.

(b) Ho: $P_2 \geq 55\%$ against H_1: $P_2 < 55\%$.

(c) Ho: $P_1 = P_2$

Where P_1 and P_2 are the ratios of lower status divorced/separated Muslim women in Murshidabad and Barddhaman respectively.

(a) The proportion of women whose husbands were not engaged in socially prestigious professions is 26 out of 58 in Murshidabad.

$\therefore\ P_1 = .4482.$

If Ho is true; expected value = 0.55

Standard error = 0.0653238

So $Z_1 = -1.5583906$.

Since $Z_1 > -1.645$, it does not fall in the critical region and we do not reject hypothesis.

(b) Following a similar procedure, we find that: $Z = -0.12$, and Ho is accepted at 5 per cent level of significance.

(c) To compare P_1 and P_2, we first calculate the estimate of the equal but unknown proportion P which is 0.5.

Standard error of $(P_1 - P_2) = 0.0887789$.

So, $Z = 1.0656753$.

Since $|Z| < 1.645$, we accept Ho at 5 per cent level of significance.

Therefore, we can form the following conclusions from our above analysis:

(i) The hypothesis that divorce among Muslim women is more prevalent among the low income group is borne out from the evidences collected in our survey. Both the districts Murshidabad and Barddhaman show a distinct positive relationship between lack of income and practice of divorce/separation among Bengali Muslim women.

(ii) Evidence from Murshidabad and Barddhaman indicate that the said practice is more prevalent among the low status group. However, there is a marked divergence between

Murshidabad and Barddhaman as far as economic conditions of the divorced Muslim women are concerned. The practice of divorce is seen to be more prevalent among the low income group in Murshidabad as compared to Barddhaman. On the other hand, there is no reason to suspect such divergence between the two districts as far as the relationship between status and divorce is concerned.

Note that we have considered only the occupations of the husbands in determining the status of a woman. Lest it should be thought that we suffer from chauvinistic myopia, we also take a brief look at the professions followed by the guardians of our interviewees.

Forty of the interviewed guardians (22 in Murshidabad and 18 in Barddhaman) were housewives----which does not tell us anything. This is most nondescript and non-informative of all occupation. Leaving aside those 40, and a further 29 guardianless divorcees, we find that 28 out of the remaining 59 guardians are in low status professions, i.e., nearly half of the relevant total figure.

Our next hypothesis is that there is a wide divergence between theory and practice regarding marriage and divorce among Muslim women. Here we examine the three broad perspectives of marriage and *talaq*, i.e., consent of the bride for marriage, *mahr* (bride money) and *iddat* (three menstrual cycles).

It is to be noted here that Islamic law makes it compulsory to obtain the consent of the bride for marriage. Her marriage depends on her approval being given on her own conditions. The proposal comes from the man and the acceptance is made on behalf of the woman by her *wali* (the marriage guardian). The *ijab* and *qubul*----as the consent of the marrying parties are called----are mandatory; though differences exist in the modalities of obtaining consent. However, our survey reveals that only 16 out of 58 parents (roughly 27.6%) in Murshidabad took the consent of their daughters to marriage. The corresponding figure for Barddhaman is much higher, nearly 71.5 per cent (the above figure relates to information provided by the divorced women themselves. When the parents were interviewed, the same question evoked a different response. However, the differences can be ignored). This is a clear indication that in Murshidabad, in particular, there is a wide divergence between theory and practice regarding marriage. Engineer[3] rightly observes:

> ...the *Jahiliyah* practice of contracting marriage by her *wali* (marriage guardian) on her behalf re-established itself and her approval was reduced to a mere nod or silence. From playing an active role in marriage she came to be relegated to a passive position.

As far as divorce is concerned, it was observed that knowledge of rules and regulations about *talaq* as laid down in the *Quran* and *Hadith* was limited to a very small group of interviewees in Barddhaman. Strangely enough, none of the interviewees from Murshidabad---all divorced/separated Muslim women---possessed any information about the religious viewpoint of the practice---indeed, a trauma---through which they had all passed.

The *Quran* is very specific on the question of *iddat* (i.e., three menstrual cycles). The condition of a woman during *iddat* is dealt with not only in *Surah Al-Baqarah*, Chapter II of the Holy *Quran* but in the *Surah Al-Talaq*, Chapter 65. The relevant provisions are as follows:

> *Surah 2, 228*
> Women who are divorced have to wait for three monthly periods, and if they believe in *Allah* and the Last Day they must not hide unlawfully what *Allah* has formed within their wombs. Their husbands would do well to take them back in that case, if they wish to be reconciled. Women also have recognized rights as men have, though men have an advantage over them. But *Allah* is all-mighty and all wise.

Surah 2, 231
When you have divorced your wives, and if they have reached the end of the period of waiting, then keep them honorably (by revoking the divorce), or let them go with honour, and do not detain them with the intent of harassing lest you should transgress. He who does so will wrong himself. Do not mock the decrees of *Allah*, and remember the favours *Allah* has bestowed on you, and revealed to you the Book and the Law to warn you of the consequences of doing wrong. Have fear of *Allah*, and remember, *Allah* is cognisant of every thing.

Surah 2, 232
When you have divorced your wives and they have completed the fixed term (of waiting), do not stop them from marrying other men if it is agreed between them honourably. This warning is for those among you who believe in *Allah* and the last day. This is both proper and right for you, for *Allah* knows and you do not know.

Surah 65, 1
When ye have to divorce women, pronounce divorce only when they are in free state (i.e., free from menses or pregnancy) ... Do not turn them out of their houses... . *Allah* may perhaps bring about a reconciliation between you.

Surah 65, 2
And when they reach their prescribed term, either retain them with kindness or part from them in a just and gentle manner. Take two upright witnesses to the transactio... . *Allah* will show a way to the righteous for an honourable reconciliation or an honourable parting.

Surah 65, 4
The prescribed term of waiting is three months except for pregnant women for whom time is extended till they have laid down their burden ... .

Surah 65, 6
Lodge them (women in *iddat*) where ye yourselves lodge and let them live in a style ye yourselves live... .

In our field study, we found that no one in Murshidabad or Barddhaman has observed the tenets laid down in the *Quran*. If we look a bit deeper into the data collected, the said divergence between theory and practice regarding divorce becomes even more marked; 53 per cent of the *talaq* in Murshidabad as per our survey had their origin in extra-marital affairs of the husband and dowry problem—the former being the dominant reason (26 cases). In Barddhaman, these two reasons accounted for 51 per cent of the divorce/separation—with the spectre of extramarital affair casting its shadow over the lives of 40 per cent (28 out of 70) of the interviewed women. In sharp contrast, the traditions of Islam do not approve of such wanton divorce.

Wide variation is also to be found in case of *mahr*. In Islam, marriage is a contract between persons belonging to two opposite sexes. The consideration of the contract is *mahr*, gift to the bride, the amount of which, not being fixed by law varies from one *dinar* upwards. Without *mahr* a marriage cannot be said to have been properly solemnised. It is the exclusive right of the woman or bride to determine the amount. And the *mahr* belongs to the wife alone. The *mahr* money has been given to the bride as a token of love, fidelity and sincerity. The *Quran*[3] repeatedly exhorts men to give *mahr* to the women. It says:

> And give women their dowries as a free gift. But if they of themselves be pleased to give you a portion thereof, consume it with enjoyment and pleasure.

Mahr is defined as a sum of money or other property which the wife is entitled to receive from the husband in consideration of the marriage (Mulla).[4] Paras Diwan[5] has contradicted this view. He criticises this definition on the ground that *mahr* is not payable "in consideration of marriage", but is an obligation imposed by law on the husband as a mark of respect for the wife, as is evident from the fact that non-specification of *mahr* at the time of marriage does not affect the validity of marriage.

Without entering into the debate, we are here concerned with finding out whether *mahr* is an amount payable by the husband to the wife on divorce. The main reason behind our confusion is that, under the Muslim Personal Law, the amount of *mahr* is usually split into two parts, one of which is called 'prompt', which is payable on demand, and the other is called 'deferred', which is payable on the dissolution of marriage by death or divorce. But the fact that deferred *mahr* is payable at the time of the dissolution of marriage, cannot justify the conclusion that it is payable on divorce.

It is usually asserted that the *mahr* is a good security for the woman in case of any difficulties in her marital life, and when she is divorced the *mahr* money has to be given to her. However, we see from our data that only two out of the 128 women interviewed got *mahr*, in spite of the fact that as many as 54 of them were divorced because of extra-marital relations harboured by their husbands. Can there be any better evidence of the gulf of difference between theory and practice of divorce in the Muslim community of West Bengal?

Levy[6] rightly observes:

> When family life is concerned, in marriage, divorce and the distribution of inheritance, the provisions of the *sha'r* would appear to be very widely neglected.

Hence, our hypothesis that there is wide divergence between theory and practice regarding marriage and divorce appears to be correct in view of the data collected in our survey.

To assess the role played by Muslim women in the family's decision-making process, a specific question seeking the opinion in this regard of the guardian as well as of the woman concerned was included in the interview schedule. The interviewees (both the divorced/separated women and their guardians) were questioned in order to measure the extent to which women are actually consulted before taking a decision regarding family matters. Apart from such direct questions, the dignity (or lack of it) enjoyed by Bengali Muslim women in the family could also be assessed from some other revealing information.

When the guardians were asked whether, in their opinion, women should be consulted before taking decisions concerning the family, all the 47 and 52 guardians in Murshidabad and Barddhaman, respectively, answered in the affirmative (remember that 11 women in Murshidabad and 18 in Barddhaman did not have their guardians). However, when they were asked whether the opinions of their female proteges were actually taken, only 38 per cent and 7 per cent of the guardians in Murshidabad and Barddhaman respectively asserted that they often did so. Another 14 per cent in Murshidabad and 28 per cent in Barddhaman admitted to have consulted their womenfolk some of the times. So only, 52 per cent of the guardians in Murshidabad and 35 per cent in Barddhaman actually consulted women before taking any family decisions.

The attitude of the guardians can also be comprehended from a brief look at question 5 (i.e., what did you hold as the thing of utmost importance in relation to your daughter's marriage?) of the interview schedule for the head of the family. Only 10.6 per cent of the interviewed women (excluding the ones without guardians) chose their own spouses in Murshidabad, while the corresponding figure in Barddhaman was 9.6 per cent. We have already seen that in a high proportion of cases, consent of the would be brides was also not taken. However, the above statistics have to be viewed in juxtaposition with those regarding the bride's age. Nearly 49 per cent of the interviewed women in Murshidabad were married off before they reached 16 years of age (as far as 47 guardians could remember), while the corresponding figure for Barddhaman was 57.6 per cent. Naturally, the guardians then felt little need to consult their 'young' words.

The situation becomes clearer when we hear from the

women themselves (the divorced/separated ones---and not the female guardians) how actively they participated in the decision making process in their conjugal lives. It is interesting to note that nearly everyone (except four persons in Barddhaman) felt the necessity of allowing women a greater says in family matters. However, when we asked them to specify the domains in which they wanted to have their way, we were confronted with a bewildering inter-district variation. While in Murshidabad, 48 out of 58 interviewees wanted to restrict the role of women to running the household (only nine opined that women should be consulted regarding all family matters of importance); only 10 (out of 70) interviewees in Barddhaman considered running the household to be a women's headache. As many as 40 of them wanted to be a part of the family 'brain-trust' in all matters of importance. This huge gap cannot be attributed to differentials in education, for, though Barddhaman had a larger percentage of literates (as per our survey), the difference is not wide enough to evoke such a diametrically opposite response.

This gap in the perception of a woman's role is perhaps the reason behind another strange piece of information that is presented in question 55 (i.e., on which points, according to you, women should be consulted?) of the interview schedule meant for the divorced/separated women. If we formed the opinion that Barddhaman had a more progressive atmosphere as far as infusing greater self-respect in women was concerned, we should hasten to retrace our steps when we confront question 56 (i.e., did your husband consult you while taking any decision?). It presents the paradoxical result that while almost the entire set of interviewees in Murshidabad (52 out of 58 or 89.6%) were consulted regarding family matters, the interviewed women in Barddhaman revealed that they were less lucky. To be precise---only 18 out of 70 (a little above 25%) of them were taken into confidence by their husbands.

However, the above statistics does not contain any paradox, but can actually be viewed as a logical culmination of the findings of question 55 (i.e., on which points, according to you, should women be consulted?). As the interviewed women of Murshidabad generally considered the running of households to be the only pasture for their grazing, they were satisfied when consulted on purely household matters. Of course, we make the realistic assumption that husbands, irrespective of religion, status and earning ability, often consult their spouses on matters involving day-to-day running of the family. After all, it is the wife who performs all the household chores. But she is left out of the decision-making process when issues like purchase of consumer durables or property crop up. The interviewees in Barddhaman perhaps did not attach much importance to purely household issues, and did not consider it a great privilege to be consulted on such matters as to which particular vegetable should grace the family menu the next day. Hence, the low percentage of affirmative answer to our query 55.

As we review the whole situation, it is very difficult to reject the hypothesis that Muslim women do not play any vital role in the family decision-making process.

Firstly, evidence suggests that the would be bride has a minimal say in the choice of her spouse. Secondly, an analysis of the joint evidence of question 54 (i.e., is there any necessity to take the opinion of women in the family decision-making process?) and 55 (i.e., on what points are women's opinions needed?) reveals that while in Barddhaman, women are seldom consulted before taking a crucial decision, it is very likely that Muslim women in Murshidabad are similarly relegated to the category of 'non-thinkers'. Thirdly, the interviewed guardians in both districts, contrary to what they preach, show greater reluctance to take the opinion of women on important family matters.

Equally important is the frequency with which women move out of their homes, their reasons for doing so and their relationship with outsiders.

From the statistics we have collected we see that the use of veil is widely prevalent among the Muslim women. Nearly all the interviewed women use the veil (only four out of 128 do not); so there is little point in having recourse to a statistical exercise to 'prove' it. On the other hand, the use of *burqa* is limited to only, a few less than 15 per cent of the total use. Interviews with the guardians also revealed a similar attitude. While 37 out of the 47 guardians in Murshidabad and 45 out of 52 guardians in Barddhaman supported the custom of *purdah*, only nine and 13 of them (respectively in Murshidabad and Barddhaman) support the use of *burqa*.

However, it would be wrong to presume from the above that they rejected the use of *burqa* out of a 'progressive outlook'; 31 of the 52 guardians of Barddhaman indicated that only financial stringency due to low income had prompted them to do so.

As far as the movement of women outside their house is concerned, it is seen that practical necessity---economic and other has led to such liberation. However, it appears that they prefer (as do their guardians) moving out only under compelling circumstances. In response to a question as to whether Muslim women should confine themselves to their homes, an overwhelming majority (94.8% in Murshidabad and 85.7% in Barddhaman) of the interviewed divorced/separated Muslim women replied in the affirmative. Their guardians also showed a similar reluctance to allow free movement to women; 93 per cent of the guardians in Murshidabad and 90 per cent of them in Barddhaman were in favour of confining their womenfolk to home. Thus, even if *purdah* cannot be literally observed, its spirit is still alive among the Muslims of Murshidabad and Barddhaman.

We have discussed the 'non-inclusion' of Muslim women in the family brain-trust, the prevalence of the use of veil and the general reluctance to allow them freedom of movement. All of these constraints can be said to reveal a scheduled status for

Muslim women. Thus, we need not go into the details again to establish that the divorced/ separated Muslim women of Barddhaman and Murshidabad and, by inference, Muslim women in rural West Bengal are secluded in general and are uneducated (or we should say that they suffer from lack of education).

Over the decades, the expansion of women's education in India has been a much debated issue among all concerned, including social reformers, politicians and policy makers. The likely influence of the formal educational system in bringing about changes in the thought process, aspiration levels and status of women was severely constrained by the prevailing notions on how a girl should be socialised.

The importance of education in raising the quality of life is well known. Indeed, the lack of it is now being recognised as one of the most formidable obstacles to development. Though the number of schools and school going girl children have increased over the years, male superiority in decision-making and control affects the self-perception of women, and also conditions of familial views on feminine role. This necessarily limits the nature and scope of change possible through education.

The gender gap in education, i.e., the difference between the enrolment ratio of boys and girls and the literacy ratio of men and women, exist in all the states of India. Most states have been trying to close the gender gap by highlighting women's issues and by seeking to provide equality of opportunity by removing all gender-based discriminations. Mahbub ul Haq and Khadija Haq[7] tried to understand the prominent features of the existing gender gaps in South Asia. According to them:

> The gender gaps are large and persistent at all levels of education in South Asia:
>
> In 1995, 50 million children did not have access to primary schools. Of these, more than half were girls.

> At the primary level, net enrolment of girls was only 69 per cent, compared to 88 per cent for boys—a gap of 19 per cent points compared to only 5 percentage points in developing countries. At the secondary level, generally girls' enrolment is half that of boys.
>
> Gender disparity in participation and còmpletion of the primary cycle further reduces the value of this education. About 42 per cent of girls dropout at the primary level in South Asia, compared to 7 per cent in Arab states. These gender gaps appear glaring when one looks at the statistics for adult literacy in South Asia. South Asia's female literacy rate at 36 per cent is the lowest among all regions of the world: it is about one-half of the average for the developing world and compares quite poorly with 48 per cent in sub-Saharan Africa and 95 per cent in East Asia (excluding China). Out of the total illiterate female population of 545 million in the world, South Asia's share is 45 per cent. South Asia is entering the Twenty-first century with 243 million illiterate women, who represent two-thirds of the total number of adult women in the region.
>
> They further argue:
>
> The reasons for gender gaps in education are many and complex and they differ from one country to another, from one culture to another. Yet, there are certain factors constraining girls' educational opportunities which are common across cultures.

Before going into further details, we need to define the concept of education. Durkheim (1956:71) defines education as "the methodological socialisation of the young generation". Later sociologists included the influence of social class background, family relationships (Craft, 1972), peer group influences, classroom interaction and the effect of social class on the construction of ability (Shimpson and Rosenholtz, 1986; Rosenbaum, 1986) as the prime areas of importance in the sociology of education. Marxist sociologists differed in their concern and emphasis from those who raised the question of ideology and the role of the state using specific Marxist framework and applied it to education (Freire, 1972; Althuser, 1971).

From this basic understanding, we may observe that education improves people's ability to acquire and use information, it helps them to better understand the social and economic environment they live in, guides them to make better choices as consumers and producers and instills confidence in them. Their productivity is improved, as are their horizon and creativity. Better educated women are also better informed about the importance of health care and personal hygiene, and "tend to be less affected by the absence of community health programmes and tend to use them more frequently when they are available."[8]

The importance of educating women is clearly brought out in the diagrams displayed on the next page.[9] These diagrams clearly show the importance of maintaining a low gender gap in education.

We all know that in independent India the practice of recording community-wise literacy figures has been discontinued. So, we do not know how far behind the Indian Muslims have fallen in literacy and education. But the fact is that educational status of the Indian Muslims, in general, and West Bengal Muslims, in particular, in contemporary period is not very satisfactory at all. It has been estimated from the sample survey that in contemporary period the literacy rate of the Muslims in India is only about 34 per cent (males 48% and females 19%).[10] From this high gender gap prevailing among the Muslim community in India (such gap is true for West Bengal also), we can legitimately infer that Muslim women are an inhibited lot, not responsive enough to new informations and ignorant of the environment around them. Regarding female literacy among the Indian Muslims, S.R. Mondal[11] observes that:

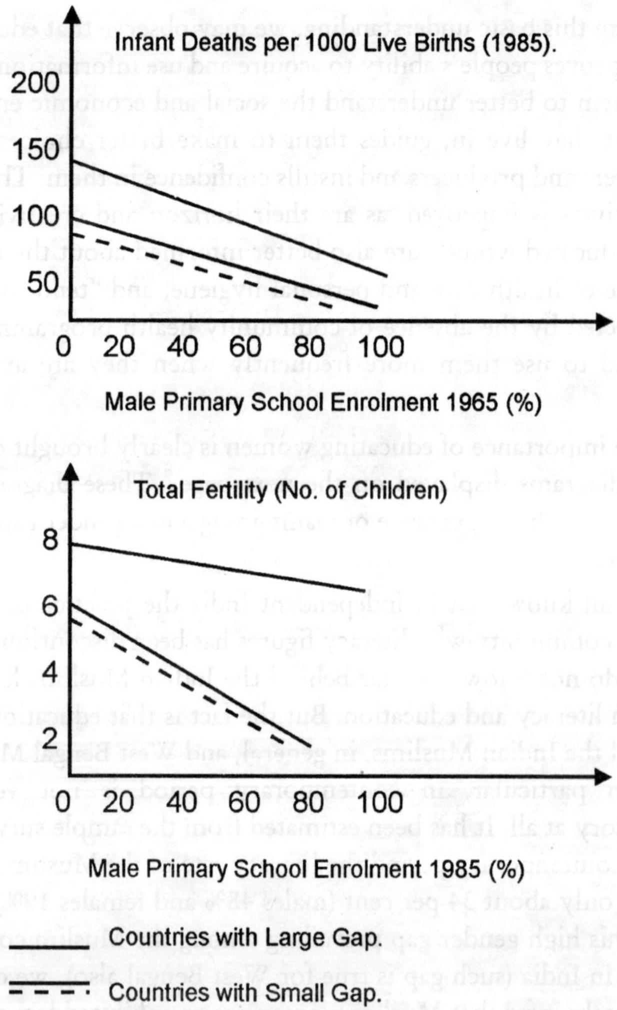

(Both the diagrams have been drawn under the hypothesis that educating women now will bear the fullest fruits 20 years from now).

> The female literacy among the Muslims is also significantly low (about 19%) and this is one of the important reason of perpetuating ignorance and illiteracy in Muslim community. Again the adult education among the Muslims (both male and female) is significantly lacking. Besides formal education, the learning of new skills and technology is also not very satisfactory among the members of the Muslim society. All these facts have shown that the ignorance and illiteracy are the characteristics of the Muslim community in India. Therefore, it is the duty of the social anthropologists and sociologists to find out the educational status and to analyse the state of education among the Muslims of various parts of the country to explore the constraints of educational upliftment among them.

The need for spreading education has also been felt by a number of Muslim scholars in the beginning of this century. Muhammed Majharul Haque[12] in an article "Islame Stree Siksha" asserts:

> The early education of a child is likely to be better imparted through the efforts of the mother. But an illiterate mother can not perform such (important) functions... .
>
> As long as we remain blind to the legitimate rights of women in respect of education, there is no doubt whatsoever that a vital organ of our society will be non-functioning.

Syeeda Khatoon[13] under the heading "Narir Sadhinata" states:

> Women constitute an integral and important part of society, and it is now quite palpable that erecting barriers in their path to development is a serious mistake. The realisation has truly dawned on our Muslim sisters that it is only because of (such) orthodox people that we are lagging so far behind our neighbouring sisters (from other communities).

If we look at the following statistics we find that education among the Muslims was not as widespread as among the Hindus. In an article 'Bengali Muslims in Education Field', *Saptahik Saugat*[14] asserts that:

Muslim total	1,29,57,775 (male)	
Hindu total	1,05,36,119 (male)	
	Hindu	*Muslim*
Primary	6,94,704	6,90,185
Middle stage		
Middle English school	65,647	15,312
High English school	82,767	14,150
	8,43,118	7,19,647
University and intermediate education		
	Hindu	*Muslim*
Intermediate class	12,621	2,051
Degree class	5,406	853
Post graduate class	1,188	99
Research student	20	00
Female		
Muslim	1,22,53,029	
Hindu	96,67,408	
	Hindu	*Muslim*
Primary stage	1,25,936	1,66,182
Middle stage	905	76
Higher stage	582	22
	1,27,423	1,66,280
	Hindu	*Muslim*
Intermediate class	94	0
Degree class	58	1

	Total Students	*Hindu*		*Muslim*	
		Boys	*Girls*	*Boys*	*Girls*
Art College	22,889	19,235	152	3,003	01
Law College	3,140	2,709	00	406	00
Medical	1,780	1,527	00	125	00
Engineering	293	294	00	19	00
Teaching	119	70	03	20	01
Commerce	548	519	00	29	00
Veterinary	137	86	00	37	00
Total	28,834	24,395	155	3,639	02

It means that Hindus constituted 85.1 per cent of the total students community, while the corresponding figure for the Muslim was 12.2 per cent.

	Total Students	*Hindu*	*Muslim*
	Boys		
Higher section	98,545	82,767	14,150
Middle section	82,973	65,687	15,312
Primary section	14,11,685	6,94,704	6,90,185
	Girls		
Higher section	1,365	582	22
Middle section	2,028	905	76
Primary section	3,01,987	1,25,936	1,66,182

If we take note of Table 7.1, we find that the pervasiveness of illiteracy among the Muslim women, in particular, and Hindu women, in general.

Table 7.1

Comparison of Education of Muslims and non-Muslims (percentage of Muslim and non-Muslim population with education)

Province	*Year*	*% of Muslim Male Pupils to Total Population*	*% Other Males*	*% of Muslim Female Pupils to Total Population*	*% Other Females*
Madras	1916	4.9	3.6	1.8	1.4
	1926	7.9	4.1	3.1	2.3
Bombay	1916	3.1	3.8	-	-
	1926	4.5	5.4	1.4	2.1
Bengal	1916	3.2	3.9	1.3	1.3
	1926	3.8	4.6	1.4	1.6
Uttar Pradesh	1916	1.7	1.6	-	-
	1926	3.1	2.5	-	-

Source: Compiled from Memorandum on Progress of Education in British India 1916-1926, Calcutta 1927, pp., 47-59.

In the light of the above discussion, we can say that the position of Muslim women in respect of education has not improved much though need for education among Muslim women has been felt early in this century. In his evidence before the Education Commission of 1882, Syed Ahmad Khan stated that in India, women were almost entirely excluded from education. He urged that English and not the vernacular be used as medium for education, and he went on to say:

> I beg to say that the general idea that Mohammedan ladies of respectable families are quite ignorant, it is an entire mistake. A sort of indigenous education of a moderate degree prevails among them. The poverty of Muhammadan's is the chief cause of the decline of female education among them.

He admitted, however, that the general state of female education among Mohammedans is far from satisfactory, but at the same time, he was of the opinion that the government cannot adopt any practical measure by which respectable Mohammedans may be induced to send their daughters to a government school for education. The fact is that no satisfactory education can be provided for Mohammedan females until a large number of Mohammedan males receive a sound education and inspire the women to have education.

The situation has remained the same for Bengali Muslim women though a century has passed. If we take note of our field data, we find that on the question of education Muslim women are lagging far behind the rest of the female population; illiteracy is pervasive among the Bengali Muslim women. According to 1991 census any person who can both read and write with understanding in any language is deemed to be literate. In the said census any child below seven years was treated as illiterate and the question on literacy was not canvassed to him/her. With this definition in mind we find from our survey that out of a total of 128 respondents, 111 were illiterate, 16 respondents had primary education and only one was matriculate.

The purpose of the above discussion is to show that the Muslim women in West Bengal cannot be expected to have a high level of aspiration due to their extremely low level of educational attainment. To have even moderate aspirations, they would need a vent through which communication with the outside world is possible. Information about opportunities, knowledge of the pros and cons involved, courage and confidence to meet possible obstacles and the ability to be equal to the task at hand—all these are required in varying degrees to have a realistic aspiration for higher goals. Lack of education and seclusion shut that very vent on Muslim women.

It is small wonder that owing to their poor educational attainment, economic condition and social status, the Bengali Muslim women in general are not eager for social mobility. People with opportunities to migrate (inter-sectoral and inter-spatial) will not accept a lower real wage or a lower status than what they normally expect to achieve. However, lack of opportunities and hence of sufficient realistic aspiration tend to imbue in people a preference for 'status quo', or to be more accurate, make them two timid to try to break the 'impasse'.

In view of our discussions we think that the hypothesis that seclusion and lack of education create in Muslim women a low level of aspiration, and this in turn dissuades them from striving for status mobility, is perfectly acceptable. Indeed, it logically follows our earlier findings.

Our next hypothesis is as follows: the traditional value system of Muslim society assigns to woman a subordinate position to men and this value system is still in operation in Muslim society.

To do justice to the above hypothesis, we shall dwell on the following aspects:

(a) What really does the traditional value system of Muslim society say about the position of women vis-à-vis men?

(b) What are the manifestations of a subordinate position?

(c) In the light of our previous discussion and results of the survey undertaken, is the above hypothesis tenable?

We may say at the outset that the traditions of a society do not always bear a close resemblance to the dictum laid down in the religious scriptures which are most revered in that particular society. Therefore, an assessment of the impact of the traditional value system of Muslim society would be incomplete if we simply look at the textual tenets of the *Quran* and *Hadith*.

Instead, we have to examine the views expressed from time to time by scholars and other persons of eminence, and more importantly, the actual practice followed over the years. What do we see from such an examination?

First, let us take a look at what Prophet himself had to say on the position of women vis-à-vis men.

The *Quran* does not place women an a pedestal which can be called equal to that of men by today's standards. However, the *Quran* was not written just yesterday, but a good many centuries ago. The progressiveness of an attitude has to be viewed in the perspective of the relevant time and space. The pre-Islamic Arabia had carried deprivation of women to an extreme level, and the *Quran* initiated a remarkable improvement in her status. The practice of killing the girl child was forbidden in the *Quran*. The *Quran* refers to it in different times.

The verses 81:8,9 talk about the wrath of *Allah* on the day of resurrection and intimate that *Allah* shall inquire on that day of the female child, who has been buried alive, as to for what sins of her was such fate meted out to her. In *Surah 16*, verses 57-59 it is said:

> *Surah 16, 57*
> They attribute daughters to *Allah*, to glorious, but for themselves whatsoever they please.
>
> *Surah 16, 58*
> Yet, when news of the birth of a daughter reaches one of them, his face is darkened, and he is overwhelmed with silent grief,
>
> *Surah 16, 59*
> And hides from people for shame at the news, (at a loss) whether he should keep her with shame, or bury her in the ground. How bad is the judgement that they make!

Women were given certain rights, and a religious leash was put on men to restrain them from perpetrating their cruelty on women.

Here, we can cite some traditions flowing from the Prophet himself which help us to establish that he was in favour of equitable and just status of women in society. The Prophet of Islam very often recommended and pleaded for kind treatment of wives, as well as of women in general. He is reported to have said:

The women ought to behave towards their husbands in like manner as their husbands should behave towards them, according to what is just.[15]

He also said to his followers:

the best of you is he who is the best to his wife (*Mishkat*, Treatment of Women).

Ye men have rights over your wives and your wives have rights over you (*Mishkatul-Masabih: Babu'n Nikah*).

When a man has two wives and does not treat them equally, he will come on the Day of Resurrection with half of his body fallen off (*Bukhari* 11:13).

The Prophet is also reported to have said:

Beat not your wives.

The Prophet asked the Muslims to treat their well, for they have taken them as a trust from *Allah* (*Muslim, Hajj*).

He said that the belief of a Muslim is complete to the extent that he cultivate good habits; and exhibits toleration to his wife (*Tirmidhi*).

The woman is the ruler in the house of her husband (*Bukh, Nikah*).

That if you have four *dinars*, spend one of them in Holy War waged in self-defence, contribute the second towards setting a slave free, give the third to an orphan and the fourth to your wife; the last will earn you the greatest reward in the eye of *Allah*; that the whole world is useful and the best of it is a good wife (*Mishkat*, Treatment of Women).

So much about the dictates of the Prophet. However, human civilisation is a melting pot and it is greatly dynamic in nature. The social opinion about a certain issue, people's attitude towards a particular problem—everything changes with time. Thus, even in early Islamic era, interpretation of the Prophet's wishes were variegated and many traditions were attributed to Him in different places in West Asia. There were local conventions so to speak—and in those pre-electronic ages, with communications of all sorts extremely hazardous to conduct, it was an easy thing to misinterpret the Prophet's sermons. There are several Arabian proverbs, which give us some insight into the status of women at that age.

One of the proverbs of the Prophet says:

> Women, houses and horses are ominous,

and the other says:

> Admonish your wives with kindness, because woman was created from a crooked bone of the side, therefore if you wish to straighten it, you will break it and if you let it alone it will remain crooked.

Still another says:

> A woman approaching from above or from behind is a form of devil (*Mishkat: Babu'n Nikah*).

Once Hazrat Abu Bakr is reported to have said:

> One who consulted woman for his affairs, would humiliate himself,

and an Arabic proverb propounds that same threat when it lays down,

> obedience to women makes one enter hell.[16]

Hazrat Ali, the fourth *Caliph*, was strongest in his denunciation of women. He says:

> Let not women remain in one state and trust them not with money. Leave them not with anything but managing the children, if you at all let them. What they desire brings you to destruction and ruin the empires. They forget good and remember only evil. They always indulge in lies and persist in insolence.[17]

Women have also been considered as the greatest *fitna*/cause of trouble in some traditions.

The religious, social and intellectual inferiority of women is also emphasised in some of the Arabian proverbs and some of them are very derogatory in nature to the female sex. These are as follows:

> The beauty of a man is in his intelligence and the intelligence of a woman is in her beauty.[18]

> Women are defective in understanding any religion.[19]

> Women have been omitted by *Allah* from his mercy.[20]

> Obedience to women make one enter hell.[21]

> The cunning of women is strong and that of the devil is weak.[22]

> When a woman becomes old, nothing remains in her but poison and colour of sulphur.[23]

However, as we have mentioned earlier, our perceptions change with time. New value judgements evolve; and though it is debatable whether value judgements can be assigned 'marks', we feel that they get 'better' with time in the sense that the hosts of value judgements prevailing in a society at a point of time become less mutually contradictory and more consistent with a broad, overall norm as the years go by. This is not unnatural with the vast increase in knowledge, which human beings have acquired over the years, and opening up of new horizons. We know ourselves and our environment better. It is but natural that under these circumstances, we should constantly 'update' our values. The great misfortune of Muslim societies is that they have consistently refused to be dynamic. In spite of the variegations of social conventions one to differences in time and space that we have alluded to, Muslim societies have still maintained a strong link to a set of value judgements which had marked a significant progress once upon a time, but are certainly not very relevant today. This is perhaps true for most religions---indeed most ideologies constituted important watershed in the history of human civilisation, but any attempt to justify the set of "do's and don'ts" enumerated in them in today's context would be as vain an attempt as challenging the superiority of a present-day telescope over Galelio's 16th century instrument. Ideas must be continuously renovated, new information assimilated and changing realities incorporated in any value system if it aspires to be a 'living' one. M. Mujib[24] says:

> And it is a matter of approach, why should Muslims confine themselves to texts embodying traditional methods of approach, and not think afresh in the light of present-day needs and realities.

In his lectures on "The Reconstruction of Religious Thought in Islam", Iqbal has pointed out:

> The ultimate spiritual basis of all life, as conceived by Islam, is eternal and reveals itself in variety and change. It must possess eternal principles to regulate its collective life, for the eternal gives us a foot hold in the world of perpetual change. But eternal principles, when they are understood to exclude all possibilities of change which, according to the *Quran* is one of the greatest 'signs' of God, tends to immobilize what is essentially mobile in its nature. The failure of Europe in the political and social scene illustrates the former principle, the immobility of Islam during the last 500 years illustrates the latter.

After a careful examination of the trends of historical development, the thinking of Islamic jurists and the basic spirit inspiring Islamic religion, Iqbal has come to the following conclusion:

> The claim of the present generation of Muslim liberals to re-interpret the foundations of legal principles, in the light of their own experience and the altered conditions of modern life is, in my opinion, perfectly justified. The teaching of the *Quran*, that life is a process of progressive creation necessitates that each generation, guided by unhampered by the work of its predecessors should be permitted to solve its problems.

And he goes on to add:

> The closing of the door of *Ijtihad* is pure fiction, suggested partly by the crystallization of legal thought in Islam and partly by the intellectual laziness which, specially in periods of spiritual decay, turns great thinkers into *idols*.

The above discussion was cast in a more general framework than the scope of the present study strictly on merits. But it is felt that this hypothesis is of a global nature and therefore warrants a broader approach than followed so far.

We shall not be overstepping our domain if we look at the following pieces of statistics for World Bank Development Report 1984 and 1991.

In presenting the above data, we consider two Islamic countries, two European market economics, one European socialist country, one South American market economy, one Latin American socialist economy and non-market economics from all over the world. All the countries belong to the upper middle income or the high income categories; so there should not have been much disparity in the basic developmental indicators. However, it is seen that in every respect Iran and Saudi Arabia are much behind the other countries and women appear to be discriminated against in these two countries. It is a notable feature that their per capita GNP are actually greater than Bulgaria

	Infant Mortality (per 1000 live birth) 1989	*Life Expectancy at Birth % 1989*	*Number Enrolment in Primary School as % of the Age Group*		*Crude Birth Rate (per 1000) 1989*	*Females per 100 Males (secondary) 1988*	*Population per Physician 1984*	*Population per Nursing Person 1984*	*G.N.P. Dollars 1989*	*Birth Attended by Health Staff% 1985*
			(a) Female 1983	*(b) * Male 1983*						
	(1)	*(2)*	*(3)*		*(4)*	*(5)*	*(6)*	*(7)*	*(8)*	*(9)*
Saudi Arabia	67	64	56	81	42	66	740	340	6020	78
Iran	90	63	88	113	44	68	2840	1110	3200	N.A.
Spain	08	77	110	112	12	101	320	260	9330	96
Bulgaria	13	72	100	100	12	180	280	160	2320	100
Canada	07	77	102	105	14	95	510	N.A.	19030	99
Cuba	12	76	105	111	18	N.A.[a]	530	N.A.	N.A.	N.A.
Astralia	08	77	104	105	15	99	440	110	14360	99
Venezuela	35	70	104	106	29	119	700	N.A.	2450	82
Portugal	13	75	123	122	12	114	410	N.A.	4250	N.A.

a The average figure for socialist economics for col. 5 is 102.

* The data in col.3 refer to estimates of total enrolment of students of all ages in primary school. The primary school age is taken to be 6-11 years, so the percentage may go above 100.

and Venezuela while Saudi Arabia's per capita GNP is also higher than that of Portugal.

It would be too simplistic to attribute their backwardness to Islamic traditions alone, but this factor cannot be totally ignored as well. The political system in those countries, structure of their economy and income distribution have no doubt played a large part in retarding their development, but the retardation, especially the educational discrimination against women, cannot be entirely unrelated to traditional Muslim values, which do assign a subordinate position to women.

It is seen from the results of our survey that the position of the divorced/separated Muslim women in West Bengal is low. In general, they come from low income families, with their guardians and husbands struggling for a hand-to-mouth existence. Not only are the income levels low, but also their families, are more often than not, engaged in the so-called low status occupations. However, since we interviewed every divorced/separated Muslim woman of the said localities, we can say that it is prevalent among low-status group Muslims, and as such it is hardly surprising that they continue to live in misery.

But their social position leaves much scope for improvement. Peculiarly enough, women are often excluded from the family decision-making process, not only by in-laws and husbands, but by their parents too. This clearly shows that they are not held in high esteem, and little faith is reposed on their thinking abilities.

Discrimination against women is, of course, nothing new to the world; it has a long history, a universal following (not necessarily only among men) and is by no means extinct. Tradition has always treated the physically weaker sex poorly. West Bengal has been no exception to the rule, and Bengali Muslims have just followed suit. Our survey attempted to find the real position as well as status of such a woman and assign causes thereof. We have found that she is a neglected creature and often a victim of discrimination and male chauvinism (recollect the high percentage of *talaqs* arising out of extra marital affairs of the husbands). It would be naive to look for a single cause—illiteracy, economic poverty and tradition (both religious and social) have all intermingled inseparably to contribute to her plight. It is like a vicious circle—one cause leads to another and there is no way out until one breaks the entire circle.

Apart from analysing the field data we may also observe that in the holy texts freedom has been given to the Muslim woman in the *Quran* and *Hadith* unlike her Hindu counterparts. It has to be noted that the Muslim woman was perhaps the first among advanced civilisations who enjoyed some rights of property inheritance. Also consent to her marriage was made compulsory and she also got the right of *mahr*. But due to her lack of education, low economic and social status, she is often not aware of all such rights. This may be due to the male dominance in Muslim society that all these rights have become meaningless to her. And then also the implication of the boundary maintenance of minority community is presenting a conservative stance. In a country like India the Muslims are primarily recognised as a distinct community through their religion and its manifestations at the level of social organisation. In a non-Islamic country adherence of a people to their religion and social system depends on the organisation of Islamic tradition. The *Quran* and *Hadith* preserve the whole content of the traditions and protect them against any kind of deviation. The Muslims are made constantly conscious of their tradition by different means like *namaz, Jumma namaz* (Friday prayer), *milad* and *jalsa*. Institutionalised facilities like *madrasah* are there in the Muslim community. For this reason, whatever freedom has been given to her in the *Quranic* texts become negative in practice. In addition to all these factors, it is observed that the network of great tradition of Islam in all these localities is interested to keep the status of women low.

Also, sources of power among the Muslims lie with rich people of the community and these rich people manage to maintain a link between the spokesmen of the great tradition and the masses. Ranjit Kumar Bhattacharya[25] rightly observes that the rationalisation of inequalities among the various Muslim social groups always serves the interest of the Muslim groups of higher status. A social group of lower rank generally refrains from making such generalisations, preferring to speak only in terms of Islamic tenets of equality. In short, it is the upper '*jat*' (caste), economically privileged and politically powerful within their society, which constitute the force which makes a positive impact in maintaining the organisation of social-cultural boundaries. They are constantly endeavouring to dislodge the secular elements of the Muslim society from the vantage position with a view to monopolising power. Until and unless the Islamic institutions become free from their clutches, Muslims will not be dynamic and the sad plight of divorce/separated Muslim women, in particular, will not come to an end. Down with the guardians of vested interests. Let Islam make rapid strides in the path of progress in the true sense of the religion.

Notes

1. B.S. Minhas and others (1991): "Declining Incidence of Poverty in the 1980's Evidence Versus Artefacts" in *Economic and Political Weekly*, p. 1673.
2. Quoted by M. Indu Menon (1981) in *Status of Muslim Women in India*, New Delhi: Uppal Publishing House, p. 29.
3. *The Quran*: 24,4.
4. M. Hidayatullah (1972): *Mulla Principles of Mohammedan Law*, Bombay: N.M. Tripathi Pvt. Ltd.
5. Quoted in *Shah Bano Case, Shariat and the Muslim Women* (Protection of Rights on Divorce) Act, (1986), published by Judicial

Department, Government of West Bengal.

6. Reuban Levy (1962): *The Social Structure of Islam*, Cambridge: Cambridge University Press.
7. Mahbub ul Haq and Khadija Haq (1998): *Human Development in South Asia 1998*, Karachi: Oxford University Press.
8. World Bank Development Report (1991): *The Challenge of Development*, published for the World Bank, Oxford: Oxford University Press.
9. Ibid.
10. S. Hamid (1985): "Educational Status of Indian Muslims" in *Muslim India*, December.
11. S.R. Mondal (1997): *Educational Status of Muslims: Problems, Prospects and Priorities*, New Delhi: Inter India Publications, p. 23.
12. Muhammed Majharul Haque (1928): 'Islam Stree Siksha' in *Saptahik Saugat* (in Bengali).
13. Syeeda Khatoon (1929): 'Narir Sadhinata' in *Saptahik Sangat.*
14. *Saptahik Saugat* (in Bengali), 11th May, 1928.
15. Quoted by S.T. Lokhandwala (1987): "The Position of Women under Islam" in Asghar Ali Engineer (ed.), *Status of Women in Islam*, New Delhi: Ajanta Publishers, p.16.
16. Shihabuddin al-Ibshihi: *Al Mustarib*, Cairo, 1330. Vol. II, p. 209.
17. Quoted by S.T. Lokhandwala, op.cit., p. 20.
18. Wastermark (1930): *Wit and Wisdom in Morocco*, London, p. 38.
19. Ibid., p.325.
20. Ibid., p.327.
21. Ibid., p.329.
22. Ibid., p.325.
23. Ibid., p.329.
24. M. Mujib (1982): *An Introductory Note to Changes in Muslim Personal Law*, Delhi.
25. Ranjit Kumar Bhattacharya (1991): *Moslems of Rural Bengal*, Calcutta: Subarnarekha, p. 151.

Bibliography

Abdalati, H. 1975. *Islam in Focus*, Aligarh: Crescent Publishing Company.

Abraham, A. and Shhukla, S. 1983. *Sex Determination Texts*, Bombay: Women Center.

Afsar, Rita. 1982. "Women's Role: The Achievement Versus Ascription Dialectic" in *The Bangladesh Development Studies*, Dhaka: Vol. XV. No. 2.

Agarwal, J.C. 1976. *Indian Women: Education and Status* including major recommendations of the Report of the National Committee on the Status of Women in India, New Delhi: Arya Book.

Agwan, A.R. 1992. *The Educational Profile of Muslim Women in India*, New Delhi: Institute of Objective Studies.

Ahmad, Saghir. 1977. *Class and Power in a Punjabi Village*, New York: Monthly Review Press.

Ahmad, Imtiaz (ed.). 1973. *Caste and Social Stratification among Muslims in India*, New Delhi: Monohar Book Service.

---, 1976. (ed.) *Family, Kinship and Marriage among Muslims in India*,

New Delhi: Monohar Book Service.

—, 1983. *Modernization and Social Change among Muslims in India*, New Delhi: Monohar Publications.

—, 1984. *Ritual and Religion among Muslims in India*, New Delhi: Monohar Publications.

Ahmad, Rafiuddin. 1981. *The Bengal Muslims 1871-1906: A Quest for Identity*, Delhi: Oxford University Press.

Ahmad, Sufia. 1974. *Muslim Community in Bengal 1884-1912*, Dacca: Oxford University Press.

Ahmed, Manzoor. 1988. *A Study of Government Policy Regarding The Educational Uplift of the Muslims and the New Opportunities Offered by the Open Universities in the Country*, New Delhi: Institute of Objective Studies.

Ali, Ahmed. 1987. *Al-Qur'an*, Delhi: Oxford University Press.

Ali, A.A. Yusuf. 1979. *The Holy Quran: Text, Translation Commentary*, Lahore: Amana Corporation.

Ali, Syed Ameer. 1902. *The Spirit of Islam*, Calcutta: S.K. Lahiri.

—, 1950. *The Ethics of Islam*, Calcutta: Christopher.

—, 1978. *Islamic History and Culture*, Delhi: Amar Prakashan. Altekar A.S.

—, 1983. *Position of Women in Hindu Civilization*, Delhi: Motilal Banarasidass.

Alvi, Hamza A. 1979. 'Kinship in West Punjab Villages' in *Contribution to Indian Sociology*. New Series.

Amal, Rassam. 1984. "Toward a Theoretical Framework for the Study of Women in the Arab World" in *Women in the Arab World*, London and Unesco: Paris: Frances Pinter.

Anderson, J.N.D. 1959. *Islamic Law in Modern World*, New York: New York University Press.

Ansari, A. Iqbal (ed.) 1989. *The Muslim Situation in India*, Delhi: Sterling Publishers Private Limited.

Ansari, Ghans. 1959. *Muslim Caste in Uttar Pradesh: A Study in Culture Contact*, Lucknow: Ethnographic and Folk Culture Society.

Ashraf, K.M. 1970. *Life and Conditions of the People of Hindustan*, New Delhi: Munshiram Manohar Lal.

Ashrafi, Talat Ara. 1992. *Muslim Women in Changing Perspective*, New Delhi: Commonwealth Publishers.

Ayub, Gouri. 1986. 'Bharatiya Musalman Samaje Ajker Meyera' (Beng.) in *Baromas*, Calcutta.

Azizah, Al-Hibri (ed.) 1982. *Women and Islam*, Oxford: Pergamon Press.

Babakhan, Z.K.I. Ishan. 1980. *Islams and the Muslims in the Lands of Soviets*, Moscow.

Bagchi, Jasodhara (ed.) 1995. *Indian Women: Myth and Reality*, Hyderabad: Sangam Books (India) Limited.

Baig, Tara Ali. 1976. *India's Woman Power*, New Delhi: S. Chand and Company.

Begum, Rokeya S.H. 1973. *Rokeya Ranchanabali* (in Bengali) ed. by Abdul Kadir, Dacca: Bangla Academy.

Begum, Shaista and S.B. Imanullah 1963. *Form Purdah to Parliament*, London: Crescent Publishing Company.

Bhattacharya, Ranjit Kumar. 1991. *Moslems of Rural Bengal*, Calcutta: Subarnarekha. Bhatty, Zarina.,

---, 1976. "Status of Muslim Women and Social Change" in B.R. Nanda (ed.) *Indian Women: From Purdah to Modernity*, New Delhi: Vikas Publishing House.

Borthwick, Meredith. 1984. *The Changing Role of Women in Bengal 1849-1905*, Princeton, N.J.: Princeton University Press.

Bourguignon, E. and others (eds.) n.d. *A Women of World: Anthropological Studies of Women in the Societies of the World*, A.J.F. Bergin Publishers.

Brijbhushan, Jamila. 1980. *Muslim Women in Purdah and Out of It*, New Delhi: Vikas Publishing House.

Broom, Leonard and Seltznick Philip. 1955. *Society*, Evanston: Paterson and Company.

Carroll, Lucy. 1979. "The Muslim Family Laws Ordinance, 1961: Provisions and Procedures---A Reference Paper for Current Research" in *Contribution to Indian Sociology*, New Series, Vol. 13. No. 1.

Chakraborty, Krishna. 1978. *The Conflicting Worlds of Working Mothers,* Calcutta: Progressive Publishers.

Chanana, Karuna. 1988. *Socialization Education and Women: Explorations in Gender Identity*, Hyderabad: Orient Longman.

Das, S. 1979. *Purdah: The Status of Indian Women*, New Delhi: E.E. Publication.

de Beauvoir, Simone. 1949. *The Second Sex*, Translated and edited by H.M. Parshley, Reprint 1974: Penguin Books.

De, Amalendu. 1982. *Islam in Modern India*, Calcutta: Maya.

Debi, Kailasbasini. 1865. *Hindu Abalakuler Bidyabhyas O Tahar Sammunnati*, (in Bengali), Calcutta.

Desai, Neera and Krishnaraj, M. 1989. *Women in Indian Society: A Reader*, New Delhi: Sage Publication.

Desai, Neera 1957. *Women in Modern India*, Bombay: Vora and Company.

Dube, Leela. 1969. *Matriliny and Islam*, Delhi: National Publishing House.

Dube, Leela and Abdul Rahman Kutty. 1969. *Matriliny and Islam: Religion and Society in Laccadives*, Delhi: National Publishing House.

Engels, Fedrick. 1973. "Origin of Family, Private Property and State", in *Selected Works*, Moscow. Vol. 3.

Engineer, Asghar Ali. 1984. "The Status of Women in Islam" in *On Women*, Special Perspective on Women: Bombay.

---, 1985. *Indian Muslims: A Study of the Minority Problems in India*, New Delhi: Ajanta Publications.

---, 1985. *Islams and Muslims: A Critical Reassessment*, Jaipur: Printwell Publishers.

---, 1985. *Indian Muslims: A Study of the Minority Problems in India,* New Delhi: Ajanta Publishers.

---, 1987. *The Shah Bano Controversy*, Bombay: Orient Longman.

---, 1987. (ed.) *Status of Women in Islam*, New Delhi: Ajanta Publishers.

---, 1992. *The Rights of Women in Islam*, New Delhi: Sterling Publishers Private Limited.

Everett, Jana Malson. 1979. *Women and Social Change in India*, New Delhi: Heritage Publications.

Fatima, Mernissi. 1975. *Beyond the Veil: Male-female Dynamics in Modern Muslim Society*, Bloomington: Indiana University Press. Freeman, JO (ed.)

---, 1975. *Women: A Feminist Perspective*, California: Mayfield Publishing Company.

Friedan, Betty. 1963. *The Feminine Mystique*, Penguin Books.

Fyzee, A.A. 1972. *Reform of Muslim Personal Law*, Bombay: Nachiketa.

Gaborieau, Marc. 1972. "Muslims in the Hindu Kingdom of Nepal", in *Contribution to Indian Sociology*, New Series 6.

Gandhi, Rajmohan. 1988. *Understanding the Muslim Mind*, Penguin Books (India) Private Limited.

Gandhi, M.K. 1945. *Women and Social Injustice*, Ahmedabad: Navjivan Publishing House.

Gauba, K.L. 1978. *Passive Voices: A Penetrating Study of Muslims in India*, Bombay: Thacker and Company.

Gettstein, K. (ed.) 1986. *Islamic Cultural Identity and Scientific Technological Development*, West Germany: Baden— Baden.

Ghadially, Rehana. 1988. *Women in Indian Society: A Reader*, New Delhi: Sage Publication.

Government of India. 1952. *Muslims in India*, Delhi: Ministry of Broadcasting.

---, 1971. *Census of India*, Social and Cultural Tables, Series 22, West Bengal, Part II C (i).

---, 1971. *Report of the Committee on the Status of Women in India*, Delhi: Department of Social Welfare.

---, 1974. *Towards Equality*, Report of the Committee on the Status of Women in India, New Delhi: Department of Social Welfare.

Guha, Uma. 1965. "Caste among Rural Bengali Muslims" in *Man in India*, 45.

Guillaume, Alfred. 1986. *Islam*, England: Penguin Book Limited.

Haq, Mushir Ul 1972. *Islam in Secular India*, Simla: Indian Institute of Advanced Studies.

Haq Khan, Mazhar Ul. 1982. *Purdah and Polygamy*, Delhi: Amar Prakashan.

Haq Mahbub ul and Khadija Haq. 1998. *Human Development in South Asia*, Karachi: Oxford University Press.

Hate, C.A. 1969. *The Changing Status of Women in Post- Independence India*, Bombay, Allied Publishing Limited.

Husain, S. Abid. 1965. *The Destiny of Indian Muslims*, Bombay: Asia Publishing House.

Hyder, Qurratulain. 1975. "Muslim Women in India" in Devaki Jain (ed.) *Indian Women*, Delhi: Government of India, Ministry of Information and Broadcasting.

Iglitzin, L.B. and Ruth Ross (eds.). 1976. *Women in the World: A Comparative Study*, Oxford: Oxford University Press.

Imam, Zafar (ed.). 1975. *Muslims in India*, New Delhi: Orient Longman.

Iqbalunnissa, Hussain. 1940. *Changing India: A Muslim Women Speak*, Bangalore: Holali Press.

Ismail, Razia. 1972. "Working Women in India: Their Problems", in *Weekly Round Table*, New Delhi.

Islam, M. Nurul. 1973. *Bengal Muslims Public Opinion as reflected in the Bengali Press 1901-1930*, Dacca.

Jacobson, Doranne. 1976. "The Veil of Virtue: Purdah and the Muslim Family in Bhopal Region of Central India" in Imtiaz Ahmad (ed.) *Family, Kinship and Marriage among Muslims in India*. New Delhi: Manohar Book Service.

Jain, Devaki (ed.). 1975. *Indian Women*, Delhi: Government of India, Ministry of Information and Broadcasting.

Jain, Shashi. 1988. *Status and Role Perception of Middle Class Women*, New Delhi: Puja Publishers.

Jeffrey, P. 1979. *Frogs in a Well: Indian Women in Purdah*, New Delhi: Vikas Publishing House.

Jones, L. Bevan and U.R. 1941. *Women in Islam*, Lucknow.

Jung, Agnccs. 1987. *Unveiling India: A Woman's Journey* New Delhi: Penguin Books (India).

Kapadia, K.M. 1966. *Marriage and Family in India*, London: Oxford University Press.

Karim, A.K.N. 1956. *Changing Society in India and Pakistan: A Study in Social Change and Social Stratification*, Dacca.

Kabir, Humayun. 1964. *Education for Tomorrow*, Calcutta ; Firma K.L. Mukhopadhyay.

Kamat, A.R. 1981. "Literacy and Education of Muslims" in *Economic and Political Weekly*, Vol. XVI, No. 23, June 6.

Kettani, M. Ali. 1986. *Muslim Minorities in the World Today*, London, Manshell Publishing Company.

Khan, M.Q. 1988. "Orthodoxy and Islam" in *The Times of India.*

Khan, Zillur. 1968. "Caste and Muslim Peasantry in India and Pakistan" in *Man in India* 48:2.

Khatoon, Syeeda. 1928. 'Narir Swadhinata' in *The Saptahik Saugat* (in Bengali).

Khan, M.A. 1984. *Muslims in the Process of Rural Development in India*, New Delhi: Uppal Publishing House.

Krishan, Kumar. 1987. *Utopia and Anti-Utopia in Modern Times*, Oxford: Basil Blackwell.

Krishna Raj, Maithrey (ed.). 1986. *Women Studies in India: Some Perspective*, Bombay: Popular Prakashan.

Lateef, Shahida. 1990. *Muslim Women in India*, New Delhi: Kali for Women.

Levy, Reuban. 1931. *An Introduction to Sociology of Islam*, London.

---, 1969. *The Social Structure of Islam*, Cambridge: Cambridge University Press.

Lokhandwala, S.T. (ed.). 1971. *India and Contemporary Islam*, Simla: Indian Institute of Advanced Studies.

---, 1986. "The Position of Women Under Islam" in Asgar Ali Engineer (ed.) *Status of Women in Islam*, New Delhi: Ajanta Publishers.

Lundberg, G.A. 1926. *Social Research*, New York: Longmans Green and Company.

Madan, T.N. (ed.). 1976. *Muslim Communities of South-Asia-Culture and Society*, New Delhi: Vikas Publishing House.

Malik, Ram. 1962. *Women in Islam*, Hyderabad.

Maududi, Syed Abdul A'la. 1992. *Purdah and the Status of Women in Islam*, New Delhi: Markazi Maktaba Islami.

M. Hidayatullah and A. Hidayatullah. 1906. *Mulla's Principles of Mahomedan Law*, Bombay: N.M. Tripathi Private Limited.

Menon, M. Indu. 1981. *Status of Muslim Women in India*, New Delhi: Uppal Publishing House.

Mitchell, Juliet and Oakley Ann (eds.). 1976. *The Rights and Wrongs of Women*, Penguin Books.

Minhas, B.S. and Others. 1991. "Decline Incidence of Poverty in the 1980s: Evidence Versus Artefacts" in *Economic and Political Weekly*, Vol. XXVI.

Mishra, Rekha. 1967. *Women in Mughal India (1526-1748 A.D.)*, Meerut: Meenakshi Publications.

Minault, G. 1982. "Purdah Politics: The Role of Muslim Women in Indian Nationalism 1911-1924" in H. and G. Minault (eds.) *Separate Worlds: Studies of Purdah in South Asia*, New Delhi: Chanakya Publication.

Mohammed, Mujeeb. 1965. *Education and Traditional Values*, Meerut: Meenakshi Publication.

---, 1967. *The Indian Muslims*, London: Allen and Unwin.

---, 1968. *Social Reform among Indian Muslims*, Delhi: Delhi School of Social Work.

----, 1972. *Islami Influences on Indian Society*, Meerut: Meenakshi Publication.

Moinuddin, S.A.H. 1996-97. "Sociology of Talak: Test and Context" in *Politics and Society*, Midnapore; West Bengal: Vidyasagar University.

----, 1998. "Women's Movement in India: Issues and Perspectives" in Anil Jana (ed.) *Indian Politics at the Crossroads*, New Delhi: Commonwealth Publishers.

Mondal, S. Rahim. 1985. "Problems of Modernization Among the Muslims: A Case Study of a Village in West Bengal" in *North Bengal University Review*; 6.

----, 1992. "Toward Understanding Islam and Muslim Society in India: Some Methodology Issues" in *Journal of Objective Studies*. Vol. 4 No. 1 July.

----, 1992. "Economic and Social Situations among Muslims of West Bengal: Some Empirical Observation" in F.R. Faridi and M.M. Siddiqui (eds.) *The Social Structure of Indian Muslims*, New Delhi: Institute of Objective Studies.

----, 1994. *Dynamics of Muslim Society*, New Delhi: Inter-India Publications.

----, 1997. *Educational Status of Muslims: Problems Prospects and Priorities*, New Delhi: Inter-India Publications.

Murshid, Ghulam. 1983. *Reluctant Debutante: Response of Bengali Women to Modernization 1849-1905*, Rajshahi: Sahitya Samsad.

Nanda, B.R. 1967. *Indian Women from Purdah to Modernity*, New Delhi: Vikas Publishing House.

Noorni, A.G. 1972. "Reform of Muslim Personal Law" in *The Indian Express*.

Noor, Y.R. 1976. 'Indonesian Women's Participation in Development' in B.B. Hering (ed.) *Indonesian Women*, Bruxellas Centre.

Radha, B.P. 1904. *A Glimse of Zenana Life in Bengal*, Anddy and Company.

Rashid, A. 1969. *Society and Culture in Medieval India*, Calcutta: Firma K.L. Mukhopadhyay.

Rodinson, Maxime. 1971. *Mohammed*, Penguin Books.

—, 1980. *Marxism and the Muslim World*, New Delhi: Orient.

Roy, A. Chandra. 1968. *History of Bengal: Mughal Period 1526-1765*, Calcutta: Navbharat Publishers.

Roy, Shibani. 1979. *Status of Muslim Women in India*, Delhi: B.R. Publishing Corporation.

Roy, M.N. 1939. *Historical Roles of Islam*, Reprint 1990, Delhi: Ajanta Publications.

Saiyed, A.R. 1976. "Purdah, Family Structure and the Status of Women" in Imtiaz Ahmad (ed.). *Family, Kinship and Marriage among Muslims in India*, New Delhi: Manohar Book Service.

Saiyed and Saiyed. 1982. "The Muslim Family in Transition: Orthodoxy and Change in a Minority Group Family" in J.S. Augustine (ed.) *The Indian Family in Transition*, New Delhi: Vikas Publishing House.

Salma, Sobhan. 1978. *Legal Status of Women in Bangladesh*, Dacca: The Bangladesh Institute of Law and International Affairs.

Sarkar, J.N. 1972. *Islam in Bengal*, Calcutta: Ratna Prakashan.

Selltiz, Johada et al. 1969. *Research Methods in Social Relations*, Methuen and Company Limited.

Sen, Shila. 1976. *Muslim Politics in Bengal* 1937-1974, New Delhi: Impex India.

Shamsuddin. 1961. 'Status of Women in Ancient India' in *Social Welfare*. Vol. VII, No. 5. Aug.

Shustery, A.M.A. 1937. *Outlines of Islamic Culture*, Revised by Dr. Fahmida Begum and Professor M.K. Ahmed Ibn-e-Makdoom, 1992, Bangalore: The Bangalore Printing and Publishing Company Private Limited.

Siddiqi, M.Z. 1971. *Sir Abdullah Memorial Lectures on the Social Position of Women through the Ages*, Calcutta: Calcutta University.

Siddiqui, M.K.A. 1974. *Muslims of Calcutta: A Study in Aspects of their Social Organization*, Calcutta: Anthropological Survey of India.

---, 1984. *Educating a Backward Minority*, Calcutta: Abadi Publication.

---, 1989. *The Quran: A Message for All Mankind*, Calcutta: Abadi Publication.

---, "Caste among the Muslims of Calcutta" in Surajit Chandra Sinha (ed.). *Cultural Profile of Calcutta*, Calcutta: Anthropological Survey of India.

Siddiqui, M.Y. 1987. *Muslim Women in Transition: A Social Profile*, New Delhi: Harnam Publication.

Singh, Alka. 1992. *Women in Muslim Personal Law*, Jaipur: Rawat Publications.

Singh, Y. 1973. *Modernization of Indian Tradition*, New Delhi: Thompson Press.

Singh, Niroz. 1989. *Woman and Violence*, New Delhi: Vikas Publishing House Private Limited.

Smith, W.C. 1947. *Modern Islam in India: A Social Analysis*. Lahore: Ripon Printing Press.

Smith, W. Robertson. 1885. *Kinship and Marriage in Early Arabia* Cambridge. Cambridge University Press.

Soha, Abdel Kader. 1984. "A Survey of Trends in Social Sciences Research on Women in the Arab Region, 1960-1980" in *Women in the Arab World*, London: Frances Pinter.

Wasserstrom, R.A. (ed.) 1979. *Todays Moral Problems*, New York: Macmillan Publishing House.

Wastermark. 1930. *Wit and Wisdom in Morocco*, London.

Weeks, Riekard (ed.). 1978. *Muslim Peoples: A World Ethnographic Survey*, Westport (Conn.): Greenwood Press.

Williams, Juanita H. 1977. *Psychology of Women*, New York: W.W. Norton and Company Inc.

World Development Report. 1991. *The Challenge of Development, Published for the World Bank*, Oxford: Oxford University Press.

Woodsmall, Ruth Frances. 1983. *Women in Changing Islamic System*, Delhi: Bimala Publishing House.

Youssef, Nadia H. 1976. 'Women in the Muslim World' in L.B. Iglitzin and Ruth Ross (eds.) *Women in the World: A Comparative Study*, Oxford: Oxford University Press.

Index